Spirit Nudges

Allowing Help from the Other Side

By

Joni Mayhan

Also by Joni Mayhan:

True Paranormal Non-fiction

Paranormal Fiction

 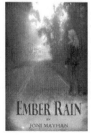 

Acknowledgements

The blank page has always thrilled me. It is a bare canvas that I can turn into anything I want it to be. I sit in front of it and imagine the possibilities before they turn into realities. My spiritual journey has been much the same.

I started out a blank page too. Through time and experiences, I've found myself accumulating knowledge and information that fits together to make a comprehensive internal manuscript, one I share freely with anyone willing to view it. I couldn't have gotten there without a steady stream of mentors, prophets and allies.

Merely saying thank you doesn't feel ample enough. These people have helped me build my foundation and continue to prop me up and fortify me with their gifts of wisdom, comfort and encouragement. I am grateful to them for everything they've done.

This list of people includes old friends, such as Psychic Medium Barbara Williams, Shaman Michael Robishaw, Sandy MacLeod, Author Gare Allen, who was also a beta reader, as well as new friends Psychic Medium Brandie Wells and Psychic Medium Crystal Folz. To all my friends in real life and on Facebook, I'm so very grateful for the stories and experiences you shared. I'm equally appreciative to my family for always keeping an open mind. I know you don't always understand what I do, but you've always been there cheering me on, regardless.

Thanks to Sue Debiasio Landry for all your fabulous suggestions and for finding my errors. Thanks also to Tami Stevens for being an early reader and to all my other readers who purchase my books and allow me to continue writing more.

Most of all, thank you to my spiritual allies for always being there to provide nudges for me to follow and allowing me to turn this blank page into something I can be proud of.

Table of Contents

Introduction

We've all been there.

The world comes down so hard on us, we want to hide in a hole until the pressure eases. We are forced to make rapid-fire decisions, but are only vaguely aware of which direction we should turn. Should I take that job and move across the country? Did I make the right decision in getting married? Should I trust my friend with this secret? What should I do?

Imagine for a minute that you have many of the answers at your fingertips. All you have to do is learn how to access them. It's not a button that you press or a file that you read; it's something that is already built into your spiritual makeup, a part of you that you might not be tuned into.

I call them nudges.

I've been getting them all my life, but the first one I truly remember occurred when I was ten years old.

I was somewhat of a willful child, one prone to pushing the boundaries. If my mother told me to be inside the house by the time it got dark, I came in mere seconds after the street lights illuminated. When I found a stray collie dog wandering the neighborhood, I hid it in our garage until I was discovered. The word no was a starting place for me, not an ending.

One night as my mother was cooking dinner, she emphatically told me that I wasn't allowed to eat any snacks before dinner. She was making fried chicken and was tired of seeing me pick at my food because I'd filled up on cookies beforehand.

As the chicken sizzled in the skillet, my mother left the kitchen to answer a phone call. Once she was gone from the room, I eyed the cookie jar sitting on the counter.

One cookie wouldn't hurt anything, right?

I had my hand out, reaching for the cookie jar when I heard a voice inside my head.

1

"Don't do that!" it said. The voice sounded vaguely like my grandmother's voice with a tone that was almost conspiratorial. She wasn't yelling at me like my mother would have done. She simply didn't want me to get caught. I dropped my arm in an instant and jolted around to glance behind me.

My grandmother wasn't there, which would have been very odd, considering she'd been dead for four years, but I wasn't alone. My mother had pulled the phone cord to the kitchen doorway and was silently watching me with arched eyebrows.

"You weren't getting into those cookies, were you?" she asked.

I feigned innocence and reached past the cookie jar to the crock of spoons. I selected the first one my trembling fingers landed on and moved to the stove, where I began stirring the boiling potatoes, my mind racing.

Who had tipped me off?

Was it my grandmother? The thought sent a chill racing down my spine. If it was my grandmother, did that make her a ghost? I wasn't sure what to make of it. The only thing I knew was that she had helped me when I needed her assistance. As it turns out, it wouldn't be the first time.

My grandmother, along with an entire army of spiritual allies, has helped me all my life. They've steered me away from bad relationships, prevented me from getting into accidents and have helped me find the path I was intended to follow. All I had to do was listen to the nudges.

It all starts with one word: *believe.*

Believe

If you are someone who only believes what you see with your own eyes, this book will be a waste of your time. Put it away and move onto the rest of your life. Come back to it when you're ready, because you have to believe before it will work.

Belief comes with an open mind, one that is willing to consider options that aren't carved in stone. You have to stretch the boundaries between what you've been taught and what you feel in your soul and allow the spark of insight a place to furrow. This is much more than Tinkerbell's magic dust, it's a concept that our minds can't fully comprehend. The world is much broader than the physical compositions we can experience with our five traditional senses.

Once you allow yourself to believe, you open up a part of yourself that provides you with access to the help you need. I think of it like a transmitter. If the switch is turned off, you won't be able to communicate. Belief is the on button. Doubt is the button that turns it all off.

Psychic Medium Brandie Wells does gallery readings several times a week in her community of Keene, New Hampshire. "I'm connecting with people in a circle and I can feel their energy. A lot of times, I know when people are blocking me or are resisting me. That resistance makes it difficult for them to receive messages. When they're already closed off, they don't understand that their resistance actually creates a block," she said.

She also feels that people don't always see the signs. "If you came in completely innocent and were taught to pay attention to these signs, you would notice them, but we're not," she said.

When we open ourselves up to a spiritual way of life, we begin to see our lives in a much broader spectrum. We begin to see the synchronicities and how they create a pathway for us to follow. We understand that the things that happen to us in our lives are lessons and not punishments. We aren't supposed to get everything we ask for. We are supposed to struggle. The more we struggle, the more we learn.

We begin to understand that everything we encounter has a purpose. Everything happens for a reason. We might see the reason immediately, but many times we never see it at all. I think of it as the Domino Effect.

The Domino Effect

Imagine this scenario. You wake up one morning and go outside to start your car. When you turn the key, nothing happens. The battery is dead.

You can't believe this is happening to you. You have so much to do at work. You can't have a delay.

You call the mechanic shop down the street and ask them to come give you a jump start. By the time you make your way to work, two hours have passed and you're late getting started. It ruins your entire day.

What you don't realize is that the reason for the delay might have actually saved your life. Someone leaving a night shift might have run a red light. Had you been at that precise intersection at your normal time, you might have been broadsided, sending you to the hospital or possibly even ending your life. Or, the mechanic you called might have been struggling to pay his bills. Your call gave him the money he needed to make a payment on his electric bill before it was shut off. Or perhaps it was due to something more personal. Perhaps, someone came to work with a fever and then left before you got there, preventing you from getting sick. Or it could have been as simple as the smile you gave someone on the sidewalk that changed their entire day.

The best way to see the Domino Effect is to look at it in hindsight.

I've had many Domino Effects in my life, but the one that stands out the clearest is the cataclysmic destruction of a dream.

After working in the pet industry for several years, I dreamed of opening my own shop. It would be small, but filled to the brim with charm. I would have handcrafted bamboo bird cages filled with colorful finches, custom aquariums shaped like coffee tables and walls filled with useful pet items. I mapped out a floorplan, found distributors to purchase my product from and even found the perfect location. All I needed was the financing.

I spent long nights pouring over my business plan. There wasn't a detail I didn't examine. I imagined myself standing behind the counter, chatting with pet owners, answering their questions. I would no longer be required to work for someone else, carrying out instructions that didn't make any sense to me. I wouldn't be forced to work the shifts that no one else wanted to work. I would make the rules and I would prosper. Every time I thought about it, I smiled. It was all I wanted.

My dream came to an abrupt end when I took my plans to the bank and asked for a business loan. They applauded me for my carefully crafted plans, but wouldn't loan me the money unless I put my house down as equity for the loan. I walked away heartbroken.

I didn't see the reason for my failure for several months. The anchor store in the plaza where I wanted to put my pet shop went out of business. Soon afterwards, nearly every store in the plaza closed as a result. Mine would have been one of them. I would have lost my house, my money and all my carefully laid out plans.

Instead, I went back to work for another company and quickly rose through the ranks, finding a place to flourish and grow, while learning the business. It was where I needed to be until I was ready to move onto another endeavor.

Last summer I encountered another synchronicity that falls soundly into the Domino Effect category. I was invited to attend an online meeting for a paranormal group out of New Mexico. I was thrilled to be involved in the meeting and met some amazing people. One of these people was Skeeter Welhouse, who shared the following story with me.

Skeeter's Story

Skeeter experienced a Domino Effect several years ago after she moved from New Mexico to Washington State. Soon after moving there, she felt compelled to join a new paranormal team in her new state. Through the experience, she was introduced to individuals on the team who embraced her abilities as a psychic medium and encouraged her to continue her studies.

Her new group members invited her to a metaphysical market, where she would conduct psychic readings for people. While she had never done public readings before, she decided to give it a try. The experience was life altering for her. It gave her the opportunity to fully explore her abilities and meet others with similar skills.

During the same time period, she opened her own seamstress business. While she enjoyed the work, it wasn't apparently part of her life's path. Soon after the Christmas season, the business began failing. Once she made the decision to close the business, her psychic endeavors began to take off. She was soon invited onto a radio show to act as the guest psychic and began getting requests from clients for paid psychic readings.

"With everything from this chain of event, I realized this was where I was supposed to go," she said. She began working on a metaphysical book and continues to do psychic readings.

"I don't know what happened, but moving to Washington from New Mexico almost a year and a half ago just catapulted me onto a path I never expected. I finally feel at home," she said.

***

Laura King also shared a story about her experiences with the Domino Effect.

Laura's Story

All my life, since a very young age, I felt I was missing my other half. I kept asking my grandma if I had an older brother who had died. When she told me no, I'd argue because I just knew it. Every so often I'd look up at the moon over the years and still feel "he" was out there, but where?

I knew there was another part of me I was missing. I gave up wondering and wanting over time. I married and had an okay life. In 1994 I became depressed and had no desire to go out anymore after losing my daughter Danielle.

While I was online one day, I saw a familiar name I hadn't thought of since 1988. It was my friend John. John and I became fast friends again and suddenly I wanted to go out. He flirted with me and made me feel attractive again. We started hanging out a few times a week. I enjoyed his company since we shared many interests. He soon introduced me to an online role playing game. I loved it and became addicted to it and became quick friends online with the guy Adam who ran it.

Adam and I started chatting and surfing the same websites online and he found this site called Cybertown. It was a 3D chat world in which you sign up and can go to different areas (they called it virtual worlds) and even take a job as a block deputy, etc., and be in charge of the chat areas. It was more complex, but I can't remember tech terms. Anyway Adam and I hung out there awhile and it felt good socializing again even if it was just online. It helped me get confidence in myself again and I felt like I could venture out in the real world.

One day when I was hosting a chat in Cybertown, this guy Michael popped up and I fell madly in love with his personality. He made me feel attractive and cared for. Long story short, I left New York to be with him in Florida. I spent 16 years with Michael, through good and bad. Michael was a good guy, but he could be somewhat abusive. Michael was disabled and couldn't earn enough money, so I had to be strong and keep jobs that overwhelmed me.

7

I learned so much in my struggles in Florida. I learned how to stand on my own two feet, what *not* to do in a relationship and what I wanted in life. One day in 2010, Michael started using Facebook. He told me it was kind of cool, so I joined.

I soon became friends with this guy Kevin on Facebook. I thought Kevin was cute but had many issues going on in his life. I quickly unfriended him, because, at the time, I had too much on my plate with Michael's abuse. I'd become depressed and had given up on relationships by this time.

Then in November of 2015, I saw a post from a friend on Facebook. As I read the responses, I saw Kevin's name. I was amazed he survived his health issues.

I was tempted to friend him, but I wasn't sure it was wise with everything I'd been through. I had a feeling we would become involved. That scared me since I felt it was going to be very intense. I didn't want the drama from another relationship. I told myself if I ran into him again, I would friend request him as it would be fate.

A few weeks later in December, I saw another posted response of Kevin's. "That's it," I told myself. I sent Kevin a friend request. It was fate.

After that, every interaction with each other was very intense. I could see in my mind's eye we were going to be romantically involved. He told me he saw it too. Long story short, we must be soul mates or twin souls. We share so much in common and we are almost exactly alike.

Kevin told me as a child, he felt he had another half of him missing and he would look up at the moon wondering where his other half was. He told me this before I admitted what I used to do. So many things we felt and did that were alike it was mind blowing. Even the length of time in both of our relationships were the same. Every time Kevin had a breakup I had one at the same time. He's 4 years older than me but we were in sync though apart and didn't know each other.

A year later, in October of 2016, I moved in with Kevin and we became engaged. If I didn't find John, who led me to Adam, who led me to Michael, and then become friends with my Facebook friend Phil, Kevin and I would never have met.

I wish Kevin and I had met earlier, but I needed all the experiences to grow as did he.

Another Domino Effect in my life was in 1985 when I wished on a shooting star for a boyfriend. I was tired of being alone. The next day, one of the workers at my job came up and asked me out. His name was Jack and we dated for quite some time. I learned a lot from him.

After I learned that Jack cheated on me with another girl, the relationship was over. Not long afterwards, I ran into the girl he cheated on me with. Her name was Amanda. We somehow ended up becoming friends.

Amanda invited me to her home where I met her sister Sara. Sara and I became fast friends and she became like a sister to me. Though she was 4 years younger, she taught me so much and opened up my life in so many ways. Whenever we went out people looked at us and asked if we were sisters.

Sara and I parted for a few years, but one day she suddenly popped back in my life. We found out we did so many similar things during that time apart, even buying the same clothes! Sara helped me realize I was in a bad marriage. She was instrumental in that too. If I didn't meet Sara, I wouldn't have had the confidence to even approach my old friend John. I don't know if everyone has as many interconnecting experiences. I am thankful for mine.

***

Laura's story showcases the steps we often need to take to reach our goals. Sometimes the steps seem more like punishments than achievements, but when you zoom out and look at them as a whole, you can see the pattern emerge.

Domino Effects come in all shapes and sizes. Some of them are so profound, it's difficult to miss them, but others are subtle and easy to miss.

Our Invisible Selves

Before we can talk about connecting with our spiritual allies, we need to spend a few minutes talking about who we are and where we came from.

I'm not talking about the place where you were born or where you were raised; I'm talking about where your soul came from.

Everyone has their own belief system. I completely respect that. I'm not here to try to convert you to some strange religion you've never heard of. I'm not trying to do anything except, perhaps, open your mind a bit wider and make you consider the possibilities.

This is what I believe.

I believe the soul is eternal. It is the driver inside your meat and bones vehicle. It is the life that propels your vehicle and makes it operational. Without it, your vehicle would just sit motionless.

Where do we come from?

For the lack of a better term, I'll call this place Heaven. It's the term that most people are most comfortable with, although some people call it the Kingdom, Source, the Hereafter, or even the Astral Plane. What we call it isn't as important as understanding its function in our lives.

It's where we all originated from and where we return to after living our lives here on Earth. In every sense of the word, it is home.

When our souls are created, they are like newborn babies. They need life experiences to help them develop. The best way to get this knowledge is by being faced with situations.

Our souls aren't just created and thrown out into the world though. We are given guardians to help us along the way. These guardians are our Spirit Guides.

Our guides help us every step along the way. They sit down with us and decide what circumstances would better aid in our development. Then, we decide what to do next.

Psychic Medium Brandie Wells also believes this. She went on to further explain the process.

"I don't believe in Hell. I believe there's a Heaven and an Earth. There are many realms, but being human, Earth is the only place where we can learn. We can't learn in any other place."

"When I'm doing readings for people, I explain to them what I'm doing and what I believe because it really is the foundation for tapping into your Spirit Guides," she said.

We Choose Our Own Parents

The first step is in deciding where we will go and who we will be born to. It might seem somewhat unbelievable to us that we would select where we will be born and to whom, but you have to remember that we aren't looking for an easy road. A road with a lot of obstacles will teach us more than one that is straight and narrow.

A lot of people resist this notion. They see themselves living crappy lives filled with towering hindrances and think, "Why would I choose something like this for myself? Why wouldn't I reincarnate into a life filled with fame and fortune?" The truth is very simple, if you look deep enough for it.

Would you truly grow if everything was easy for you? It's through our mistakes and our misfortunes that we learn the most valuable lessons. Use the rear view mirror approach and look back at some of the things you've gone through and you'll see the steps that brought you to where you are now.

Here's a good example for you. I have always struggled to make ends meet. There has almost never been a point in my life where I've made enough money to keep myself afloat. Just like most of you, I see people with so much more and I want that. I want the nice car, the nice house, the ability to live without the constant worry about bills. That would be so very blissful, but it's apparently not part of my life path yet.

After I wrote my first book, I was on such a high. All the reviews were complimentary and many people commented that it would make an excellent movie. That sole thought pretty much launched my dreams.

I imagined myself moving into a bigger house, doing book tours and sipping margaritas on the deck of my yacht. Life would be much easier and far different from the reality that I currently find myself in.

If I'm honest, I can now look back and appreciate all the things that I've done since that point. It helps me understand the reasons why I didn't find my fame and fortune earlier. If my first book had hit the best-seller's list and was made into a movie, I would have gone in a different direction. I wouldn't have tried so hard to keep going. I wouldn't have written the books that I wrote after that. I would have gotten lazy and complacent. I wouldn't be where I am right now, writing this book.

Everything we go through in our lives has a reason and a purpose. We live our lives and learn what we're supposed to learn. When the time comes, we leave these bodies and return to Heaven.

Heaven is a place of depth and love. If we've already lived other lives, we are reunited with loved ones who have passed before us and we reconnect with our spiritual allies who have been guiding us throughout our lifetime. We review every aspect of our life with our allies and grade ourselves on our experience. This process isn't done with a heavy hand and a smack on the knuckles, it is done with love and understanding.

13

Perhaps you struggled with addiction your entire life and never found a way to conquer the demons. In your life review, you would see the opportunities you had to better yourself and understand what you should have done instead. You would then watch the impact this had on everyone surrounding you and the ripple effect it generated. You would have understood that our lives have more impact than what we see in front of us. Everything we do causes a change, whether we see it or not. Our actions affect other people and can alter their lives as well as our own lives.

We are allowed to spend as much time in Heaven as we feel is necessary. If we want to learn something, instruction is provided. If we want to check on our loved ones to see how they're doing, that is our choice. Heaven is like a docking station for us to land on.

Once we're ready, we're allowed to reincarnate into new lives. We choose the situation we want to experience and we once again choose the parents we want to raise us. We do this so we can become stronger and better souls.

Veil Amnesia

When we are reborn into new bodies, our souls go through a process called "veil amnesia," where we forget everything that happened to us in our previous lifetimes. This gives us a chance to make the changes honestly. It's like being given a test to retake without the benefit of having taken it once before. This way, any positive changes we've made are a true testament to our soul's ability to develop and evolve. Our Spirit Guides are there for us every step of the way, helping us.

Besides our Spirit Guides, we also make the journey with others. We call these people our Soul Group.

Soul Groups

Have you ever met someone you felt an instant connection to? After you meet them, you feel as though you've known them all your life, even though you are basically strangers.

We feel comfortable with them, which prompts us to bring them into our circle of trust. Chances are good that these people are members of our soul group, people we've reincarnated with before.

Members of a soul group resonate at the same frequency. This frequency is how we find one another. We choose to be together again in our next incarnations. We stay together, incarnating in the same area to help one another with our voyages.

Not all soul group members incarnate at the same time. We might meet them every other lifetime or we might see them more frequently. Either way, we are inexplicably drawn together by circumstances that often feel like fate or destiny. Once members meet, there is an instant feeling of familiarity. Someone who might have been your daughter in one life, may be your father in the next.

Types of Soul Groups

There are various levels of soul groups. You might find yourself reincarnating with the same people, over and over again, while others appear less frequently.

My friend Duckie DuBois shared a story with me that I think you'll enjoy.

Duckie's Story

Our grandson is only one year old but we saw the most amazing thing when my husband and I went to meet him at the hospital for the first time. His little face lit up with recognition!

Every time we were with him up until he was maybe six months old, he did the same thing. But he got more intense like he was trying to tell my husband something. It was crazy to watch. My husband, whose names is James, (our grandson is named Jameson), would say to him, "Were we the James gang? Tell me where the gold is hidden?" We turned it into a joke because it was just so weird. Now he loves his papa so much and his face lights up every time he sees him but you can tell it's different. The memories must have faded but they have a great connection.

Duckie messaged me later to tell me of a funny synchronicity that happened shortly after she shared that story with me.

"While I was waiting at the hospital today for my test, I was reading your book. Then when I went in for the CAT scan, the technician's name was Joni. I thought that was funny."

***

Was it a strange coincidence? Or was it a sign to let Duckie know that she's on the right track? These are some of the ways our guides work to provide us with insight.

Like everything else in our lives, there are hierarchies and categories. It would be a shame for everything to be simple, wouldn't it? We have groups that so strongly resonate with one another, they couldn't miss a single lifetime together, while others pop in on occasion for various reasons.

Primary Group

This is our inner circle of souls. They will reincarnate with us more frequently, claiming a closer place within our lives. They also have the greatest influence on us. These people might be our family members, best friends, or spouses. We typically will have several members of our Primary Group reincarnating with us for each lifetime.

When I met my friend Sandy, there was an instant connection. Even after we first met, we felt as though we had been friends for much longer. As it turns out, we had been. After doing a past life regression, Sandy learned that we were brother and sister in another life. I'm certain if we did more regressions, we would see many more lives where we connected.

Sandy has been instrumental in my development as an intuitive. Since we both began developing our abilities at the same time, we were able to help each other. It makes me wonder how many other times we've helped one another.

Pam Howell frequently attended the Paranormal 101 classes I taught in Gardner, Massachusetts. During my class on past life regressions, we did a group meditation session to help us connect with our past lives. She learned that her mother was once her grandmother.

Interestingly enough, several other people in the class recognized one another during the regression. One person recognized me as his mother in a past life and someone else recognized another class mate as a sibling.

Secondary Group

These are the people that impact our lives, but not as closely as those of the primary group. They might be close friends who we share a common bond with, but aren't in our lives on a daily basis.

During our lifetimes together, we might come into one another's lives at specific times when we need the connection. This makes me think of a childhood friend I once had. We spent every waking moment together during the summer months, but grew apart as we got older. Will she pop into my next life as a beloved teacher or the neighbor who brings me chicken noodle soup when I'm ill?

Karmic Partners

These people come into our lives for brief periods to settle a karmic debt incurred in a previous incarnation. They either teach us a lesson or we teach them one. These aren't always positive situations. Sometimes a karmic debt is paid and sometimes it is earned. If you abused someone in one life, you might reincarnate with that same person in another life with reversed roles to settle the debt.

Karma is essentially a scale that must be balanced. If you did something bad in one life to someone, you will need to eventually pay it back to balance that scale. Sometimes the karmic debt is settled in the same lifetime, but other times, it takes more time.

Author Sam Baltrusis had a past life regression done years ago and learned that he was a female in a past life and was stoned to death because of infidelity.

"I kept having dreams of walking past a movie theater and a group of men throwing rocks at me and spitting at me. The name of the movie on the marquee was French (so I am thinking French Guiana). But I was holding a baby," he said.

In this situation, it's possible that he was paying a karmic debt for a transgression done in a previous life. Or, if you flip the coin, it could go the other way too. Is someone else currently paying off a debt in this life because of what they did to Sam in his former life?

Twin Flame or Soul Mates

Some believe that our souls are split at the time of creation and that our other half will also reincarnate. While they don't always reincarnate at the same time, when they do, the results are astounding. This person is your other half and you complement one another in every detail.

I was once told by a psychic medium that my soul mate died before I was able to meet him in this lifetime. This made me think about something that happened to me when I was a teenager.

I was supposed to go on a blind date with a man whose name I've long forgotten. I was unusually excited by the prospect and was counting off the days until we'd go on our date. Something about him was alluring, even though I hadn't actually met him yet. Sadly, days before our scheduled date, he died in a car accident.

I mourned his loss for years. This always felt strange to me because I was essentially mourning someone I never met. After talking to the psychic medium, I had to wonder if he was my soul mate.

I recently made a new friend who is a talented psychic medium. She told me that I have a man who is with me in spirit who identifies as my soul mate. When she told me this, I thought back to the message I received years ago. Was he really the one? My new friend blew me away with her next words. She told me that he died in a car accident before we were able to meet.

If I use the rear view mirror approach on this, I see the reasons why we weren't allowed to meet. I've been alone, for the most part, for most of my life. Even during the times when I've had a partner, there's always been a large part of myself that I've kept aside. It's what has pushed me to accomplish everything I've done. If I had someone there to support me my entire life, I wouldn't have been so compelled to work so hard. I learned far more through my struggles than I would have with someone by my side.

Whether this is true or not is up for debate. I will say that I've yet to meet someone who feels like my other half, so it might yield some truth. Think back on your life. Is this something that has happened to you?

Identifying Members of Your Soul Group

1. You feel an instant reaction to this person.
2. You feel like you know them, even though you've never met.
3. You have many things in common.
4. Chance seems to bring you together.
5. There is a certain magnetism about them.
6. They come into your life at an important period.
7. You help one another in monumental ways.

How Do We Recognize One Another?

It's a difficult concept to perceive. If you think about how large the world is and how many people are crawling around on the surface, it seems like the odds would be insurmountable that we would somehow find one another.

Some people believe that members of the same soul group resonate at similar vibrations. Since "like" attracts "like," those vibrations act like homing beacons to one another, whether we are aware of them or not. Others feel that the encounters are intentional, that our Spirit Guides make the arrangements for us to reconnect. I think it's probably a combination of the two.

Bobbie Anderson shared a story with me that demonstrates how souls might recognize one another.

Bobby's Story
At my former job we'd gotten a new boss, a young guy in his late twenties. I was in my mid-thirties at the time when he first appeared on the scene. I had a feeling "something" was up, but I didn't know how it would play out.

I asked myself if it might be that I was supposed to date him, but I didn't really feel that way about him. He may've sensed something too. A number of times when I was walking home from work, especially if the weather was bad, he'd always "just happen" to be driving by and he'd offer to give me a ride home, like he was rescuing me.

One day, I walked into the office and as I was heading further inside, he came walking in my direction to go to leave the building. Just as we were about to pass by each other, we both stepped into a shaft of sunlight streaming in through the window. As we did, we both paused because something magical happened.

I suddenly saw us in what was apparently a past life vision. We were in some royal palace. I was a high born lady, not the queen but perhaps a lady-in-waiting. He was, I felt, a knight. I'm not sure whether he was wearing armor but that's the position I felt he had. I sensed that he was like a chivalrous fan of mine.

I didn't feel like we were lovers. There were two or three other people in the room also. I had on a long dress with an empire waist.

When I came out of the vision, my young boss was looking at me with sparkles in his eyes as if he was suddenly enchanted by me.

He said, "Wow! What was that?!" I was too stunned to say anything. We never discussed what had happened. He left the job not long after and I lost touch, but I feel sure that he very possibly experienced the same vision I'd had.

I feel that as he was sort of a servant to me in that past life, he also was being of service to me in this one. That also makes me think that a person doesn't have to be in your family or even a close long term friend to have shared past life experiences with you. It could still be considered a sort of "soul family" experience. He possibly experienced the same vision I'd had.

***

Chris Anthony has also had several experiences of reincarnation, involving people she's currently close to. She feels that she and her husband have been together in many lives. She's also reincarnated with several friends. "We can't get away from one another," she said with a smile.

When I asked her how she knew they had shared past lives together, she said, "A costume may trigger something, or a picture of a place. I saw a picture of a tree in a graveyard once and had a meltdown, remembering carrying the body of a friend off after a battle to a secret location to be buried." She feels that she tends to be a warrior of some sort in most of her lives, which is good because some of them have been quite harrowing.

"My only caution is there may be stuff you can't unsee," she told me. "Depending on how many times you've been around or what type of lives you tend to have, it could be difficult."

Not All Souls Reincarnate

If you've read any of my other books, you know that I have had frequent interactions with ghosts. They come to me on a constant basis.

Think back to my earlier story about the person with the addiction problem. Imagine what would happen once he found himself at the end of his life. He made some mistakes and he hurt some people. When he sees that white light open up to him, he might panic a little bit.

What if I'm not going to Heaven? What if this white light leads to Hell instead? He might balk in that moment. He doesn't have the greater understanding of life because he hasn't been to Heaven yet. He hasn't met with his guides to see his life review and he doesn't understand how every obstacle was a lesson. He simply sees the mistakes.

If he trusts in the process, he will go through the light and move onto the natural path that we're all supposed to take. If he doesn't, he will turn around and choose to remain earth-bound. This choice leaves him vulnerable. He is now a soul without a body, which is almost like having an engine without benefit of a vehicle. He would be able to see the world around him, but not be able to interact with people. This would make him a ghost.

If he had gone into the light and made his way to Heaven, he would have become a spirit.

As a paranormal investigator and intuitive, I often encounter this. I once investigated a location and came in contact with a female soul who haunted the building. People who came into the house often felt an overwhelming sense of sadness. Women felt this especially strongly.

Throughout the investigation, by using a combination of paranormal equipment and mediumship, we learned that her name was Sara and she had been a prostitute. She didn't cross over because she felt she wouldn't be welcomed in Heaven, considering the things she did when she was alive.

We spent some time talking with her. We told her that God loves her and that he understands why she did what she did. It's part of the human condition, part of the learning experience we all go through during our human lives.

She ended up crossing over. The experience was very moving for all of us, considering how long she had been earth-bound, trapped by her own self-doubt. Once she moved along, we felt a sense of calmness come over us. Her pain had ended and she was able to continue on with her soul path. The haunting at the location subsided and life went on normally for the living.

A big reason why I do what I do is to help these souls. I recognize them as people, just like you and me. They simply didn't follow the path they were supposed to take. Whenever possible, I work with them to help ease them back onto their path so they can continue on.

The reason why I went into such great detail about this is because there is a difference in how ghosts interact with you.

A spirit has received divine instruction from his Spirit Guides and angels. He understands the bigger picture and has let go of all the human emotions and motivations that he once lived with. He can be trusted.

A ghost doesn't know anything more than what he knew when he walked the earth. He still hangs onto all the beliefs and struggles he had when he were living.

When you find yourself feeling a nudge, it's important to know that it's coming from a source you can trust. Ghosts give similar signs as spirits, but the information isn't as trustworthy.

The dead often influence the living in ways we don't immediately recognize. We'll feel a strong tug to do something or become overwhelmed by an emotion we don't understand. It gets very confusing if you don't understand the source of the information.

I once helped a person who was overcome by sudden depression. She wasn't someone who had ever had depression issues before, but became inexplicably withdrawn and filled with sorrow after investigating a paranormal location.

I suspected that she had a ghost attached to her because I've seen this sort of thing happen before. I reached out to a psychic medium friend who was able to remove the attachment and her life became normal again.

My point in telling you all of this is to demonstrate how important it is to know who you're talking to. People have found this out the hard way after using Ouija Boards as prophets, only to learn they were talking to someone with much darker intentions.

We'll get into that in a future chapter, but first let's talk about the positive influences – your spiritual allies.

Your Spiritual Allies

Don't think of your spiritual allies as babysitters. They are far more than that. They accompany us throughout all of our incarnations, helping us along the way. They aren't there to solve all of our problems, but they can provide guidance when we need it.

Spirit Guides also don't fall into a "one size fits all" category. There are different ranks and levels, each having a different purpose. Some of these guides will be with you for your entire life, while others will come and go when a lesson is needed or guidance is required.

Primary Spirit Guides

These guides remain with you for the duration of your physical life. They are the managers of your spiritual team, insuring you have the right guides for the right situations. These guides know you well and always have your best interest at heart.

Some people have one primary guide, while others will have two or more. I have been told by several psychic mediums that I have two primary guides, a man and a woman, but I only feel the woman. In many ways, I believe he stays in the background, while the female takes the lead.

I first met my female primary guide during a guided meditation. The instructor brought us into a light meditative state and instructed us to walk along a path that wound past a river. We were then told to follow a trail into a forest where we would see sunlight streaming through the trees. In that spot, we would see our Spirit Guides.

As I mentally came around the corner, I saw a woman standing in the sunlight. She looked a lot like Glenda, the good witch from *The Wizard of Oz*. She was dressed in a bell-shaped pink gown that was covered with sequins and glitter and her hair was golden blond. On top of her head was the kind of crown you'd expect to see on a princess. She told me her name was Kira.

In some ways, I believe I manufactured her image because it was what I expected to see. Over time, she has evolved to a more contemporary appearance. She now wears the same sort of jeans and t-shirt apparel that I often wear, but the feeling is the same.

She often comes to me in times of need, providing me with comfort or advice when I need it most.

Most of the time, she guides me by providing me with gentle prompts towards what I'm supposed to be doing, but sometimes I hear her clearly in my mind. My experience with my kitten Charlie demonstrates this perfectly.

During one of my trips back to Indiana, my stepmother found a two-week-old kitten sitting in the middle of the road. I volunteered to take the kitten and bottle feed him. I named him Charlie.

When Charlie was four months old, I knew I needed to get him neutered, so I brought him to a nearby clinic that offered low cost spay and neuters. I was running low on gasoline, but didn't want to be late in picking him up. There was a gas station in the same town where I was driving to. I would just fill up my gas tank after I picked him up.

The weather outside was typical of New England in the winter. The roads were coated with an icy slush and my windshield wipers beat a steady tempo as they attempted to keep my windshield clear. As I pulled up at the clinic, the freezing rain began falling harder, followed by tremendous gusts of wind.

I picked up Charlie, who was still groggy from his surgery, and brought him to my car. I drove down the street to the gas station, only to discover it had closed. The next closest gas station was over twenty miles away.

According to my car's mileage gauge, I had fifteen miles until I hit empty. What was I going to do? If I ran out of gas, I'd have to leave my car in pursuit of a gas station. I tried my phone, thinking I'd call a friend to help me, but was dismayed to see that I didn't have service in the remote location I was driving through.

I slowed my speed down as I watched the miles tick off. Charlie was more than just a pet to me. After spending several months bottle feeding him, he felt more like an offspring. I couldn't imagine leaving him in a cold car while I hiked down the road in pursuit of gas.

Suddenly, I heard a voice in my head. "You'll make it to the gas station. Just relax."

The voice was so clear and soothing, I found myself following her advice. I relaxed and eventually made it to the gas station without running out of gas.

I've had many other encounters with Kira over the years, but this one always comes to mind when I think of the times she's truly helped me. This is one of the ways our guides help us, by providing comfort and wisdom when we need it most.

Dusty Bennett's spirit guide is an Indian warrior. "I have only started seeing him recently, but I have always felt him in my emotions. For example, he will stand over my left shoulder. When he places his hand on my shoulder, I get very intense emotions. I will cry or smile out of nowhere. It usually happens when I am upset. It comforts me and makes me feel like I am not alone," she said.

Many others are surprised by what their guides look like, if they're lucky enough to see them. Cheryl Phillips found this to be true. "Although I have been involved in the Native American community for over 25 years, being the mom of half Native American kids, my spirit guide is not native. Mine is a feminine form that looks white and wears a hijab, like Mary M.," she said.

Protector Spirit Guides

They are the keepers of your past and the protectors of your future. They hold the key to the records of your soul and insure you are presented with opportunities to help you grow stronger. They also work to allow or block entities from reaching you, always looking out for your best interest.

Perhaps the greatest example I could give of a protector guide comes from my experiences with Shaman Michael Robishaw, the subject of my 2015 book *Ruin of Souls*.

Michael's protector guide is an imposing Native American who not only assists Michael, but often helps other people as well. Michael's strong connection with his guides allows him to send them out to people who are being attacked by negative energy. While most people's protector guides aren't as strong as Michael's are, I'm thankful that Michael's guides look out for me on a frequent basis. When I feel a negative entity swoop in, which happens to me far more often than normal, I contact Michael. He remotely sends in his guides and they banish the entity to a place where it can't harm others.

Master Guides

Having a Master Guide around can be very rewarding. They have a very high vibration and can be available for others at the same time they are helping you. They often appear in the form that you need them for and provide you with guidance for finding the solution to your problem. For example, if you need assistance with a particular task, a guide will often be provided for you. If you need comfort, you might see this guide as an angel. They often appear to you in dreams, meditation, and by leaving signs for you to find. They typically come and go as needed, depending on the lesson.

Master guides are often specific in nature. If you have a teacher guide to assist you with logic, this guide will have little interest in helping you with relationships.

I had a friend who was studying for her nursing degree. She confided in me that she was having a difficult time with the material and was fearful she wouldn't make it through her courses. I suggested that she meditate and ask to be connected with her master guide. She followed my advice and ended up sailing through the rest of her classes.

When I began painting pictures again, I asked for a Master Guide to help me and soon found myself hearing instruction inside my head. At first, it was difficult for me to comprehend that it wasn't simply my own internal thoughts I was hearing, but as the session continued, this skepticism abated.

"Your paint is too dry. Add more," I heard in my head.

I am one of those people who will keep something until it's past the point of being useful. I hate wasting anything, so this information was alien to me. I tried using the old paint, but my Master Guide was correct. It was too dry.

The lesson continued throughout the painting until I got to a point where I was comfortable working on my own. At that point, I thanked the guide and dismissed him to go help someone else.

Ascended Masters

An Ascended Master is someone who has lived a multitude of lifetimes and has achieved great goals as a human. They raised their vibration to a place where they no longer need to reincarnate and now assist the living.

According to Psychic Medium Barbara Williams, "They can be at many places at once. They act as superintendents of spiritual growth. They at one time lived as humans and had such grace and helped so much, they became Masters. St. Germain was one."

Family Guides

These are family members who have passed on, but remained behind to assist you in your journey. They could be a grandmother who you knew or an ancestor who died well before your birth. They have an interest in comforting you and helping you along your life path.

According to Psychic Medium Brandie Wells, "Your past loved ones become your guides." She feels that they work with their living loved ones. "They're always helping align things for us," she said. She also feels that they often send us signs.

"I've seen a lot of loved ones send messages with pennies, dimes and quarters," she said. She has also seen feathers sent as signs, but suggests people pay attention to the kind of feathers they find.

"If they find a crow feather, that is a sign of wisdom, family and intelligence. Different feathers represent different messages," she said.

In my case, my grandmother Nanny has been with me for my entire life. As I described in my book *Signs of Spirits – When Loved Ones Visit*, when I was six years-old, she came to me in a visitation dream several days after she died to say goodbye to me. She also saved me from a potentially horrific car accident when I was a young adult. People who can see her tell me that she's fiercely protective of me.

Jon Almada shared an especially poignant story with me about his grandfather.

Jon's Story

My grandfather came to help my father before he passed. It was three years of constant spirit contacts and events warning us before Dad would have seizures. We learned really quickly that if we saw an uptick in sightings of spirits in the house, Dad was on the way to a seizure and we'd load him up and head to the hospital.

I know my grandfather was behind it all because I asked for his help during the worst of the seizures in 2009. Within a week, we were having non-stop events in the house. It is something I am writing about in my own book as well.

It was remarkable and it truly was an act of love from the other side. I was so comforted by it.

I did have a lot of contact from Dad after he crossed over. I saw him the day after he passed. He walked right by me and then dissipated into nothingness. Then, we had two years of knockings and seeing him go around corners as we entered rooms. He came through for a medium we saw and she picked me out of the lineup and told me he was right there and described him perfectly. All the while, the light over me was flickering constantly. It was truly heartwarming to hear from him and know he's doing A-Ok over there. My Dad is one amazing father. It didn't hurt that my mother and I are mediums and see and sometimes hear the other side.

***

Jon's story reminds us that love knows no boundaries. Even the passage of death doesn't separate us from those who love us.

Verna Smith also shared a heartfelt story with me. It was one that brought me to tears.

Verna's Story

I have been told that my mother's father is always at my right shoulder, protecting me, but my real experience was with my deceased grandson that was accidentally run over and killed by my van.

His little brother got it into neutral and it rolled down the driveway and killed him. He was 5 years-old at the time. Since his death, he has visited me quite often and still does. I hear from him almost every night.

He caresses my cheek at night as I lay down to sleep. I have an EVP of him telling me that it was not my fault and that they were playing race car. To this day I still have a hard time with it and I always will, but his little brother suffers, not understanding that it was an accident.

***

31

Verna's story illustrates how people often feel their family guides in various ways. Some might connect with them through dreams, relocated items or scents, while others rely on physical reassurances that give us a sense of peace. Your deceased family members use what they know will resonate with you.

Joy Guides

Imagine having guides whose sole purpose is to help you find joy. If requested, they will assist you in discovering the lighter side of life. They can be almost childlike in their need to make you laugh. They help us find the beauty in life and encourage us to appreciate the happy moments instead of focusing on our problems.

I think that joy guides are one of the hardest to determine. Mine often feel similar to my primary guides. They are the ones that help me see the world's beauty and prompt me to notice it, even when I don't want to. They urge me to get out of the house, even when I'd rather stay cocooned on my couch.

One of my former students had a joy guide who was quite amusing. He was a Brooklyn man with a strong New York accent, which helped my student identify him easier. He often provided my friend with funny quips and interesting insights on the current events.

Animal Guides

Animal Guides are also sometimes referred to as Animal Totems. These guides aren't necessarily former pets in a discarnate state, but are true Animal Guides, sent to deliver us messages and help us along our path, depending on the issues we're currently confronting. Shamanism, the oldest healing tradition, believes that Animal Guides are provided to you, depending on what you need.

Animal Totems come to us frequently to deliver messages. If we pay attention to them, their assistance can be quite valuable.

Shortly before I started my *Winter Woods* fictional trilogy, I struggled with my main character's identity. I knew she needed to have an animal companion, because I feel that animals are beneficial to everyone, even fictional characters. One morning as I sat down in front of my keyboard, I was astounded to see my backyard filled with crows. There were probably thirty or forty of them crowded into the narrow lot. Most people would have been startled to see so many crows, but I was elated. I would write a crow into my story line! It ended up being the perfect addition. People who read my trilogy often comment on how much they loved Poe.

Duckie DuBois has also had an experience with an Animal Totem. She woke up in the middle of the night to discover a huge black wolf standing beside her bed. At the time, she was struggling with direction in her life. The wolf's appearance assured her that she was following the correct path.

For Brittany Macomber, her Animal Guide, who is an owl, comes to her when she needs comfort or protection. She often feels it sit on top of her head. "It happens when I'm doing healings for people and also happened when I was on a walk at night and started to feel uneasy," she said. Knowing it was there made her feel instantly safe.

Dusty Bennett's Animal Guide comes to her when she needs him. "My Spirit Animal is a large white wolf. Anytime I feel uneasy about something he will show up and I instantly feel at ease," she said.

If you have an animal show up unexpectedly in a situation that feels profound, research it online and find out what this animal means. There are many websites dedicated to the meaning behind suddenly seeing different types of Animal Totems. As you read them, also consider what this animal means to you personally.

When I see dragonflies, it connects me to my goals and makes me feel that I'm on the right path. Someone else might remember a memory they had of seeing dragonflies and connect with that memory. Someone who is fearful of insects would take away a different message from someone who has studied them all their lives. Dig deep and think about what this Animal Totem means to you.

As you read this chapter, you might feel overwhelmed by all the assistance you have access to. Besides Spirit Guides, we have deceased loved ones and animal totems to guide us along the way. While those are excellent resources, perhaps the best one is the one you carry inside yourself: your invisible self.

Your Higher Self

Imagine tapping into all that knowledge you have gained through previous incarnations. Your soul might have traveled through dozens, if not hundreds, of lifetimes, collecting a plethora of information that you can tap into.

You probably connect with your Higher Self frequently, but don't realize it. It is the pure essence of who you are. It's your thoughts, dreams and goals that are buried beneath the circumstances you find yourself in. Sometimes this information comes as a simple knowing. You just *know* what you need to do. Other times, it comes as a gut feeling. When this happens, ask yourself, "Which road should I take?" The first response that comes to your mind often comes from your Higher Self. Listen to it.

Angels

The topic of angels could consume another entire book. Some people exchange the title of Spirit Guide for Guardian Angel, but the two are different.

By definition, an angel is a spiritual being who acts as a messenger of God, but angels mean something different to everybody. According to the Bible, they are non-human beings who cannot die and cannot be numbered. They have no gender and are normally invisible, appearing only when they choose to appear. Depending on your religion, an angel will mean something different to you.

There is an entire hierarchy system for angels. They are divided into three triads. The first two triads concern themselves with Heavenly business and group order. The third sphere is where we find angels who will work with us. This group consists of Archangels and Angels.

Angels are always willing to help us. All we need to do is ask for help when we need it. Sometimes they appear on their own when we need them most, but it never hurts to ask for their guidance.

Angels' frequency is far higher than our own. When we raise our personal vibration, we ascend to a higher spiritual level, giving us easier access to our divine guardians.

Angels come to you in various ways. Sometimes they come through messages or dreams, and other times they appear as visual signs that we can translate into the message we're supposed to be receiving. Often, their signs are very similar to that which your Spirit Guides send you.

You might feel your angels in many of the same ways you feel your spirit guides. For me, they feel stronger. I hear and feel their messages louder and clearer. Others see signs of angels in the sudden appearance of rainbows, butterflies, number sequences or in unexplained sparkles of light.

Archangels

Archangels are divine beings with enormous purpose. They are considered to be in a higher hierarchy than regular angels.

Most religions agree on seven Archangels.

Archangel Michael

Archangel Michael is known as The Great Protector and is the leader of the other archangels. Many view him as God's enforcer of law and judgment. His largest goal is to cut through the veil of our fears to better connect us with our source.

He is often depicted wearing medieval armor, ready for battle. He is the warrior we often call on to keep us protected. We can call on Archangel Michael to help us cut the energy cords that have grown between us and energy that no longer serves us.

SAINT MICHAEL THE ARCHANGEL, DEFEND US IN BATTLE. BE OUR PROTECTION AGAINST THE WICKEDNESS AND SNARES OF THE DEVIL. MAY GOD REBUKE HIM, WE HUMBLY PRAY; AND DO THOU, O PRINCE OF THE HEAVENLY HOST - BY THE DIVINE POWER OF GOD - CAST INTO HELL, SATAN AND ALL THE EVIL SPIRITS, WHO ROAM THROUGHOUT THE WORLD SEEKING THE RUIN OF SOULS. AMEN.

Above is the prayer to Saint Michael the Archangel.

In my line of work as a paranormal investigator and documenter, I use this prayer frequently when I need his assistance. I use it so frequently; I have it taped to the front of my refrigerator for easy reference.

Archangel Gabriel

Gabriel means "God's Strength" and he is considered to be God's special messenger angel. Several times in the Bible he is given the job of coming to earth to provide important announcements. Some also believe he is sent to us to open channels inside of us for the purpose of creativity. He helps us with our emotions and strengthens our bonds with nature.

According to Psychic Medium Brandie Wells, Archangel Gabriel often helps me in my writing. When I feel as though my words are coming from another source, he is the one I should credit.

Prayer for Archangel Gabriel

Archangel Gabriel, It is my wish to be of service to the world. I ask you to help me to communicate with love, clarity and understanding.

Above is the prayer to Archangel Gabriel.

Archangel Raphael

Raphael is considered to be the Angel of Healing. His name translates to "God Heals." He is the guardian of the human body, assisting with emotional, physical and spiritual healing. He also helps us with personal growth and transformation.

People who are ill or are in need of emotional or mental strength should call on Archangel Raphael to help them.

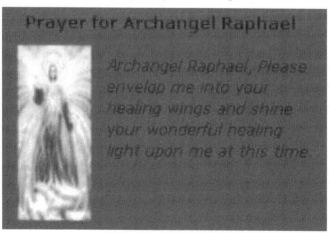

Above is the prayer for Archangel Raphael

Archangel Uriel

Archangel Uriel is the "Light of God." He guides us with new beginnings and is often symbolized by the color green and the season of spring. He helps us with anything involving rebirth.

I often have a difficult time emerging from my comfort zone. New experiences and places make me nervous. When I feel this, I call on Archangel Uriel to help me find the strength and courage to push through. He always reminds me that nothing is ever as bad as it seems.

Prayer for Archangel Uriel

Archangel Uriel, Thank you for filling me with the divine trust of God, thereby relieving me of all self-doubt and fear. May your presence help me resolve any challenges I might face, restoring order and faith in my life.

Above is a prayer for Archangel Uriel

Archangel Zadkiel

If you've done something you aren't proud of and need forgiveness, you should call on Archangel Zadkiel for assistance. His gift in the angelic realm is to help people find forgiveness, as well as forgiving others. He comforts us as he helps us heal from emotional wounds. Archangel Zadkiel also helps us mend broken relationships by bringing us together and showing us the love behind our unions.

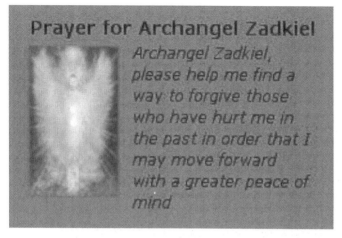

Above is a prayer for Archangel Zadkiel

Archangel Jophiel

Archangel Jophiel is the "Angel of Beauty." She is the one who helps us see past the ugliness in the world and find the true beauty hidden beneath it.

Call upon her when you need to understand how valuable you truly are. She can also help you find inspiration and fight off negativity.

Prayer for Archangel Jophiel

Archangel Jophiel, I ask for your help and encouragement to give me the motivation to clear my life and home of all unnecessary emotional and physical clutter

Above is a prayer for Archangel Jophiel

Archangel Chamuel

Archangel Chamuel is the angel of unconditional love and inner peace. If you're having a difficult time, you can call on him to help you find peace and clarity. He can also help you find lost items, much like Saint Anthony.

If you feel you need to better yourself, whether it involves finding a better job or a more satisfying relationship, Archangel Chamuel can help you with this as well, providing it's in line with your Higher Self's goals.

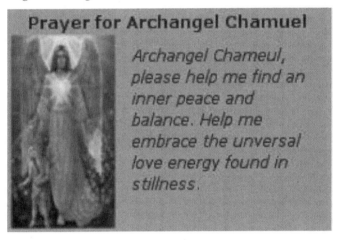

Prayer for Archangel Chamuel

Archangel Chameul, please help me find an inner peace and balance. Help me embrace the unversal love energy found in stillness.

Above is a prayer for Archangel Chamuel

Your Higher Power

Depending on your religion, you might believe in a higher power. In my case, I believe in God. Others might worship the God and the Goddess or Buddha. Despite your faith, if you believe in a higher power, you can reach out to them as well.

Over the centuries, people have relied on their faith and belief to get through tough times. The power of prayer is a potent tool and I would never discount it. Putting your belief behind something empowers it and gives it strength to assist you. You should always use the methods that resonate with you. It doesn't matter what name you give to them, only that you believe in them and allow them to help you.

Other Allies

I have a friend who worships many allies and reaches out to them, depending on their ability to assist him. One ally that he talked about was a Domovoy.

The concept originates in Slavic mythology, but it was something that felt right to me. In his teachings, each building or house develops a "house spirit" over time. It is something that watches over the property and its occupants. When I was going through an especially harrowing paranormal encounter, he suggested that I reached out to my Domovoy and ask that it keep my house and property protected.

Although this book primarily deals with your interactions with your Spirit Guides, it doesn't hurt to look at all the possibilities. The spiritual world is vast and illusive for most of us. If we narrow it down to only the aspects we believe in, we might miss opportunities and options.

If you're still having concerns about connecting with your spiritual allies, perhaps you need to build a stronger foundation first, so the communication comes easier. The first step for this is to remove the obstacles that hinder you.

Removing Obstacles

Learning how to connect with your spiritual allies involves quieting your mind enough to allow the contact. Their messages are often very subtle. It's like trying to hear a whisper in a crowd.

You can't always eliminate all of the obstacles, but you can remove some of them. Much of this involves rewinding yourself back twenty years.

Remember the days when we didn't have cell phones glued to our hands? We didn't have the need to be entertained constantly. We gave ourselves time to ponder and muse. We allowed ourselves thinking time. We were more present in our actual lives. We lived in the "now."

Part of becoming more connected to Spirit involves becoming more aware of where you are right at this moment. Set your book aside for a moment and just look around the room. Notice the things around you. Look out a window and see what's going on. Look at the details, the colors, the smells.

If you want to take this one step further, give yourself a day off from electronics. Read a book, take a walk or talk to the people who surround you every day. Pay closer attention to nature. What are the trees doing right now? Are they lush and green or bare against a solemn sky? Allow yourself to consider everything those trees have witnessed over the past decades.

I hate old cliché phrases, but "stop to smell the roses," has a haunting resonance for me. Most of us spend too much time in our own heads. As we drive to work or walk down a sidewalk, are we actually seeing what is in front of us or are we thinking about everything that is going on in our lives? There have been many times when I've found myself pulling into my driveway with only the faintest knowledge of how I got there. I put myself on "auto pilot" and dove into the thoughts in my head, allowing them to replace all the wonderful details I missed in the real world.

If you really want to embrace your connection with Spirit, try this experiment. Once a day, put down all of your electronic gadgets, including your music, and go for a walk.

Instead of humming along to your favorite song, listen to the way the wind blows through the trees or the hum of traffic as it zips along the wet streets. Listen to the birds as they sing to one another. Feel the fresh air as it goes into your lungs, cleansing you.

Nature is a great healer. A walk through the woods can ease the soul like nothing else if you are open to the possibility. Trees emit great healing energy. Allow yourself to soak it in and recharge. As we've connected ourselves to technology, we've disconnected ourselves from nature. By removing that healing aspect, we not only reduce our body's ability to refresh itself, we've replaced it with something that isn't good for us.

Electromagnetic Energy

Miranda always felt uneasy in her basement, especially near the doorway that linked the two rooms together. When she stood there, she felt as though someone was watching her, causing the hairs on the back of her neck to rise. After a while, she avoided the basement as much as possible, believing she had a ghost lurking down there.

When she called me, I was happy to help. As a paranormal investigator, that's what I do. If I find signs of a haunting, I attempt to document the activity and then work with several psychic mediums to help me alleviate the anguish that is causing the haunting. The very first thing I do though is look for normal, natural reasons for the activity.

Many people in the field call this process "debunking." While many investigators are eager to capture evidence they can share with their friends, serious investigators always rule out everything else before they label it "haunted." In Miranda's case, not only did

I debunk the haunting, but I might have saved her life in the process.

As someone who is sensitive to paranormal energy, I can tell in a matter of moments if a house is haunted. I hear a tone that is similar to ear ringing that alerts me, which is often followed by a clairvoyant "mind picture" that gives me more information. In Miranda's case, I came up empty. I wasn't picking up on anything supernatural to be causing her to feel the way she did.

I'm not one of those investigators who carries a suitcase full of equipment with me to investigations. I have a few carefully chosen pieces of equipment that I like, and I carry them in a small camera bag that I can slip over one shoulder. My favorite device is an EMF meter. I think of it as my debunking tool.

An EMF (Electromagnetic Field) detector is a device that measures electromagnetic energy, which is a type of low frequency energy that radiates from electrical and electronic devices. Paranormal investigators believe that ghosts can manipulate this energy as a sign of their presence and often use it as a communication tool. While I have seen this phenomena first-hand, my primary reason for using an EMF meter is to determine if the haunting is caused by something more dangerous than a ghost.

As I moved around the basement, the level on my EMF meter stayed at zero, which means it wasn't detecting any electromagnetic energy fields, ghosts or otherwise.

"Good so far, "I told her.

"Check near that doorway," she told me from the safety of the other room. It was obvious from the expression on her face that she was still frightened of the basement.

I moved to the doorway, watching in surprise as the numbers on my meter spiked upwards. By the time I got to the doorway, my EMF detector hit 200 mg (milligauss).

"Oh wow!" I moved around the edge of the doorway and found myself in front of an electrical panel. I didn't really need an EMF meter to see that it had been sloppily wired. It looked like a box of worms all screwed together. I called her over to show it to her.

"You need to get this fixed immediately. It's a fire hazard," I told her. It was amazing that the house hadn't already burned down.

Most people don't realize that electronic and electric devices that emit high levels of EMF energy can impact your health and spiritual well-being. People who are sensitive to the energy will often feel uneasy, as though they are being watched, and could even develop headaches and hallucinations if the EMF levels are high enough. Furthermore, EMF energy has also been linked to serious health concerns, including cancer, birth defects, Alzheimer's and depression, just to name a few.

Common items that frequently emit high levels of EMF waves include alarm clocks, refrigerators, microwave ovens and even Wi-Fi units. Research also suggests that EMF affects the pineal gland, which regulates the secretion of melatonin, which is a hormone that regulates our sleep, as well as being a natural cancer fighter. People with reduced amounts of melatonin are more susceptible to breast and ovarian cancer, prostate cancer and melanoma cancer. It has also been connected to issues with depression and even suicide. Not only can high EMF affect your connection with Spirit, it can also threaten your life.

How to Reduce Your Risk of High EMF

Check your house with an EMF meter and either remove or repair any issues you find.

Insure that all electronic and electric devices are at least 3 feet away from your bed. This includes alarm clocks and cell phones.

Make note of places in your home that make you feel uneasy. Inspect those areas for potential problems.

Don't stand in front of the microwave while warming up food and avoid using electric heat blankets unless you have tested them for EMF levels.

Another friend who suspected a haunting, had two faulty air purifying units in her living room. Each one emitted over 100 mg of EMF and were situated at either end of the room. After we discovered them, she removed them and the sensation of being watched went away immediately, as did her frequent headaches.

If you suspect that something in your house is generating high EMF energy, check it out immediately. The health concerns are far too great to ignore it.

Disconnecting Periodically From Other Humans

Another factor that might be an obstacle for connecting you to your spiritual allies is other people.

That might sound odd at first, but really think about it. How many times have you been deep in thought, only to be pulled out by the ping of your cell phone, telling you that you have a message? Or as you're attempting to calm your mind, someone calls to you from another room. Sometimes, these human interactions can be good for us and are beneficial in keeping us grounded, but other times they act more like deterrents.

Do you have someone in your life who constantly requests your attention? Their frequent communication feels more like being poked and prodded. You might find yourself living their life more than you live your own.

In the paranormal community, we call those people psychic vampires.

Psychic Vampires

The term itself is a bit daunting. When you read it, your mind might conjure up images of traditional vampires, ready to suck you dry. The truth is a bit less dramatic. There are people who pull energy from other people, much like fictional vampires drink their victims' blood.

Many of these psychic vampires aren't aware of what they're doing. They feel the need to be connected with other people, pulling them into their constant drama. This person might be a coworker who constantly needs help with projects or a close friend who needs you to solve all their problems, after listening to every detail first. Or, it could be a family member who always seems to find themselves ensconced in trouble.

The best way to determine if you have one of these people in your life is to evaluate how you feel after you've spent time with them. Do you feel drained? Is your energy level lowered to the point where you need to find another distraction to take your mind off of them? Do you find yourself sometimes allowing their call to go to voicemail or let a text message sit for a while before responding to it?

In my younger days, I had a friend who fit squarely into this category. At the time, I didn't know what a psychic vampire was. I only knew that whenever she called me, I felt agitated and tired afterwards.

This person was a pure drama queen. She couldn't live without some sort of catastrophe running through the fabric of her life. She was in a bad relationship. She was fighting with her mother. She hated her job and thought that her boss was unfair to her. Her neighbors were jerks and her children were out of control. Every time she encountered something like this, she felt the undying need to tell me about it. Sometimes the calls went on for hours without her every once asking how I was doing.

Over the duration of my life, I've discovered that I am a magnet for these kinds of people. They are drawn in by my quiet nature and my energy, almost as though they hope to absorb some of my calmer qualities. In truth, they are.

Psychic vampires pull in some of our soothing energy and exchange it with the spiky erratic energy that fills their bodies. After spending time with them, they feel calmer, but we feel more agitated. It's an exchange of energy.

I tried to "fix" my friend. I listened to all of her problems and tried to offer solutions, but the problems never ended. As soon as one issue was eradicated, another one popped up in its place. I came to realize that my best means for saving myself was to remove her from my life.

I didn't compound the situation by telling her a half-truth. It would have been easy to explain my sudden departure by telling her a lie. I could have told her that my job was becoming more demanding and I didn't have time to chat. Or I could have told her that I was currently working on a book that needed more of my time. Instead, I offered her the truth. I couldn't deal with her issues any longer. She needed to find a way to make her life happier and I wasn't the person to do it for her.

As can be expected, the friendship ended swiftly after that. I was no longer there to provide her with a quick fix, so she moved onto another person who would give it to her.

Truthfully, I believe I hung in there a lot longer than I should have. Instead of giving all my time and energy to someone who drained me dry, I could have given that to my kids, my marriage, my family or even to myself.

After she was removed from my life, I found myself feeling better about myself. My life had been returned to me. I now had time to think about my own concerns and the energy to do what I wanted to do.

My friend Kelly Spangler also had an occurrence with a psychic vampire.

Kelly's Story

"I had a friend who would constantly complain or need advice. I would be okay with allowing her some company or giving her advice. I soon noticed the more I was with her, the more drained I would feel and my own life started to crumble around me. My work load was light, I was sick all the time; I had mood swings and so on. After a few years of this, I decided I had enough. Once I let go of her, I had more energy, found more work, got a man and felt happy again," she said.

***

Margaret Florio also had an encounter with a psychic vampire.

Margaret's Story

When I first started my job, I didn't know a soul. A woman reached out to me in friendship and I was grateful. We took an exercise class together; we took our coffee breaks together and ate lunch together.

Over time I noticed she was a very unhappy person and she often complained about her job. She did not get along with her coworkers. She said bad things about them behind their backs. I did my best to be sympathetic and supportive until I realized that she was the problem.

A childhood friend of hers started working in a nearby building and we would all three go for walks together. Sometimes we would all go out for lunch. We had some fun times.

About three years ago, she went on extended sick leave without telling me. I asked her coworkers about her and found out that way. I continued to walk with her friend daily and we became close. Her friend was positive and very kind.

I got a call one day from this psychic vampire saying that she would be out for a while and didn't need anything from me. It was very curt and formal. In the meantime, I noticed I was feeling less stressed and more positive. I felt happy and content in my job.

I didn't find out she was back at work until she had been back for a week. When I finally saw her, all she did was complain. I made a sarcastic remark and she hasn't spoken to me much since. We are no longer friends. Unfortunately, her childhood friend never calls me either. I guess you have to take the bad with the good.

***

Another friend shared a story with me, but asked to remain anonymous. I will only share his first name.

Bob's Story

I work for a man who owns a good-size local store. It is a small business, so he keeps on eye on things. He tends to bring his personal life to work and gets hot headed at times. Sometimes he will rip into workers for 15 to 20 minutes in front of customers, using very insulting, intimidating tones and body language. When he storms away, you are mentally and physically drained. A few minutes later he will walk by you and talk to you as if you were his best friend.

***

In Bob's case, he can't simply remove this person from his life. Many people have this same issue, so alternative means must be employed to prevent yourself from becoming drained. There are ways to protect yourself.

The first method is insuring that you are fully grounded.

Grounding

When we hear the term "being grounded," we often think about people who are easy-going and are fully present in their lives. This isn't far from the truth, but being grounded goes even deeper than what you see on the surface.

If you consider us energetic beings, which we are, you can compare this to how electrical energy flows through a circuit. It has to be grounded before the energy can move fluidly through the channels. It's almost like turning off a light switch. The energy only travels to the point where it's shut off. When we ground ourselves, we allow the energy to flow freely and move the excess energy to a place where it won't impact us. I use it frequently during the day to help me remain calm and focused.

When I find myself in crowds of people, especially during the holidays, I make sure I'm grounded and protected before I even leave my house. All that erratic energy bounces around the building and you can't help but get caught into the web. By grounding, I can reduce the effects.

Psychic Medium Brandie Wells said, "High emotion is a block because when emotions are high, you are ungrounded. When you're ungrounded, you're not in a place to receive. Energetically, you're not in a place between Heaven and Earth, a conduit of energy, which is where you need to be in order to be a receiver or a messenger. You have to be in the same place as Spirit to receive."

Signs that you are ungrounded:

- Feeling disoriented and overwhelmed
- Have a strong need to get away from other people
- Finding yourself daydreaming and losing touch with reality
- Being agitated or feel a sense of anxiety
- Craving sugar and starches
- Inability to focus

How to Ground Yourself

Learning how to ground yourself is one of the easiest metaphysical practices to master. It might take you a little time to figure out what works for you, but once you get the hang of it, the results are worth the effort. Here is the way I ground myself.

- Imagine a white light above you.
- With every breath, pull the white light into you, through the top of your head.
- As you exhale, imagine the white light pushing negative energy down through your feet and into the ground. Some people visualize themselves as trees with deep roots going into the ground when they do this.

Other methods of grounding:

- Trees can be helpful for grounding, as well. Many people ground themselves by hugging trees and imagining the negative energy sinking into the ground beneath them, being swept away by the roots.

- Walking barefoot outdoors often helps some people to ground. Having the direct contact with the earth seems to be helpful in removing the toxins.
- Meditate and ask your Spirit Guides to remove the negative energy. Imagine yourself being purified with every breath of air you take until you feel light and happy.
- Burn sage and allow it to cover every part of your body, including the soles of your feet. Imagine the smoke clearing away all the negative energy, replacing it with clean, fresh joyful energy.
- Grounding stones such as hematite, black tourmaline, tiger eye, onyx, jasper, green aventurine, just to name a few, are helpful to assist you in grounding yourself.
  - Hold the stone in your hand and envision it empowering you.
  - Take deep breaths, focusing on the stone in your hand.
  - Imagine the stone absorbing all the excess emotions.
  - Carry the stone in your pocket during the day and hold it when you feel the need to ground.

My friend Leslie Rose grounds herself in a similar manner, but adds in another layer.

Leslie's Method of Grounding

I was taught a wonderful way to ground myself when I went to massage school. You sit down somewhere on a chair with your feet on the floor. You close your eyes, breathe in deep, and then exhale slowly. As you inhale, you imagine white light coming into your lungs. As you exhale, you imagine that white light being pushed down through your feet into the floor, where it forms root.

You keep inhaling the white light and exhaling slowly. You take your time with this and don't hyperventilate!

As you do this, you push those roots further down, through the floors beneath you, through the earth until they find a very, very large, warm rock. You envision those roots now wrapping around that rock tightly, anchoring you firmly to the earth. Now you inhale and exhale and as you do, you surround your body with a nimbus of white light that gently holds and protects you. Now you are grounded.

***

One friend, who I'll call Mary, told me something that made perfect sense to me. "I drink a lot of water to help with weight loss and to keep me healthy. I know this is going to sound unusual, but I feel like I'm grounding when I'm getting rid of all that water later when I go to the bathroom," she told me.

Her suggestion was enlightening for me. When we ground ourselves, we remove all the negative influences in our life and send them somewhere where they can become recycled into the universe. The simple task of elimination is a perfect example of this, providing you use a simple visualization method along with it. As you eliminate all the waste from your body, imagine all the negative energy and excess influences flowing through your body at the same time.

Another friend, who also asked to remain anonymous, said that sex is a great grounding tool for her.

As a culture, we're often shy about talking about things like elimination and sexual satisfaction, especially when we're linking it to spirituality. Other cultures embrace these natural bodily functions and use them to their highest benefits. I believe that if it works for you and doesn't hurt other people, then try it. Be open to the possibilities.

A large part of becoming grounded involves raising your personal vibration.

Raising Your Vibration

Everything on this planet vibrates. It might look as though we're standing still, but we are all made up of energy. The rate of our vibration will determine what types of energies are drawn to us. If we are sick or depressed, we will vibrate at a lower frequency than we would if we were happy and content.

Imagine that vibrations are a deep body of water. At the top of the water, the vibration is very high. The sun is streaming into the water, giving the water a beautiful aquamarine blue tint. As the water goes deeper, the light fades and the vibration is much lower.

As you swim in this body of water, your Spirit Guides and allies attempt to keep up with you, but the top of the water is where they are more visible. It's the place where they have the most influence over your life and where you are more visible to them.

The deeper you go, the harder time you will have connecting to your higher vibrational allies. They become almost invisible to you in the darkness. You will need to swim to the top to be able to see them more clearly.

Your vibration changes moment to moment. If you stubbed your toe, received an unexpected bill in the mail and then got into a fight with your significant other, your vibration will be low. When it's low, you attract other low vibrational energies. The term "in a rut" has a deeper meaning.

When you find yourself resonating at a lower vibration, it often feels like you are a magnet to bad experiences. The unexpected bill and the fight might be followed by being disciplined at work or having your car break down. People who allow themselves to wallow in this lower vibration continue to bring in bad energy. It surrounds them like a cloud.

You know people like this. We all do. They constantly announce each travesty on social media and insist upon telling you about it every time you see them. If you spend too much time with them, you might find yourself experiencing some of the same "bad luck" they have had.

Getting out of this rut isn't easy. It takes dedication and awareness. You have to completely change your outlook on every aspect of your life. You have to become that person who stops complaining about all the bad things and become someone who focuses on the good things instead.

You might have gotten an unexpected bill in the mail and had a fight, but what else happened that day that was positive? When you woke up that morning, did you feel healthy? Were you able to get out of bed and attend to your day? Was your breakfast nourishing and satisfying? Was the sun shining?

Chances are, there was probably a beautiful sunrise or a kind word from a friend that you missed. That's human nature. We often focus on the bad things instead of looking at the good. In doing so, we put our energy behind the negative, which gives it more power.

When I worked retail, I could have fifty nice customers go through my line as a cashier, but the only one I remembered at the end of my shift was the nasty one. I'm not alone here either. We all do this unless we change our focus.

Instead of fixating on that nasty man who argued with me over every price and complained that he couldn't find anything in our filthy dirty store, I began thinking about the nice lady who complimented me on my necklace or the man who thanked me for helping him.

I happened upon a phrase that soon became my mantra and helped me raise my vibration. It revolves around being grateful.

Practice Gratitude

Why would the Universe give you anything more if you don't appreciate what you have? That one phrase changed my entire outlook. I began to employ a "glass half full" philosophy instead of always noticing the half empty glass. I began to see the good aspects of my life and put my energy behind them. I began to always look for the bright side. I might have stubbed my toe and had a fight, but I made it to work on time and witnessed a beautiful sunrise along the way. Through doing this, I increased my vibration, which brought me to a higher plane of existence, one where my Spirit Guides existed. Once our vibrations matched closer, communication wasn't an issue.

Raising your vibration is a mindset that is influenced by the circumstances that surround you. It would be easy for me to tell you to "just be happy," but we all know this is something that is easier said than done.

It is something you have to work on. You have to adopt a "glass half full" mentality and learn to make it your mantra. For everything going on in your life, focus on the aspects that are going right instead of the things that are going wrong.

Find activities that bring you the most joy and try to work them into your life as much as possible. Remove the aspects of your life that make you sad, angry or depressed.

Once you are able to find a good balance, you will discover that life is much better at a higher vibration. Since "like" attracts "like," you will soon find yourself surrounded by blessings. My grandmother always told me, "You'll catch more flies with honey than vinegar." I don't know why anyone would want to catch flies, but the gist of the story resonates with me. If you want to attract goodness into your life, you'll have a much better chance of doing it if you are trying to lure it in with positivity.

The more you think about something, the more powerful it becomes. Thoughts make an impact on our daily lives. Would you rather empower them with thoughts about the things you want or would you rather fuel them with the things you don't want?

Ways to Raise Your Vibration

Raising your vibration basically revolves around doing the things that make you happy. The list below is not all inclusive, nor could it ever be. What resonates with me might not resonate with you. If you want your own list, sit down and write down the things that bring you joy and try to fill your life with as many of them as possible on a daily basis.

- Music and dancing
- Spend time in nature
- Exercise that you enjoy
- Give and receive hugs
- Being creative
- Practice Gratitude – be thankful for what you have
- Laughter
- Sunshine – open those blinds!
- Spend time with positive people
- Spend time with pets and animals
- Aromatherapy – fill your space with good smells!
- Focus on solutions not problems
- Get enough sleep
- Start your day with a positive mind set – it's going to be a great day!
- Eat healthy foods
- Declutter your space
- See and appreciate something beautiful (sunsets, paintings, the face of a child, etc.)
- Do something nice for someone else without any expectations of being recognized for doing it
- Remove toxic people from your life
- Meditate frequently
- Stop doing things that drain your energy. Learn how to say "no."
- Breathe deeply
- Ground and shield yourself when needed

Ways to Lower Your Vibration

Sometimes, it's difficult to avoid these lower vibrational factors. Life has a way of throwing them at us. It's how we deal with them that makes the biggest difference.

Do you latch onto them and allow them to remain in your space or do you look at them as opponents that you need to fight?

Personally, I look at them as opportunities to grow stronger. I recognize them when they appear in my life and then immediately set out to find ways to either use them for my own purposes or eliminate them completely.

Stress is by far the largest drain on your vibration, but what is stress?

In the dictionary, stress is defined as a state of mental or emotional strain or tension resulting from adverse or very demanding circumstances.

It's how we react to being overwhelmed. If it's allowed to fester in our lives, it could lead to mental and physical illness. It will take everything good in your life and turn it to mush. There is simply no way of becoming spiritually inclined if you're living in a pit of stress.

Stress comes in many other flavors. Here are some of the factors that might lower your vibration.

- Negative emotions and thoughts
- People who bring you down
- Clutter and unclean spaces
- A schedule that is too demanding
- A poor diet and lack of exercise
- A job you hate
- An unhealthy environment – too much noise and air pollution
- Not enough sleep
- Mental or physical illness
- Negative rants on social media
- Bad circumstances beyond your immediate control

There was a point in time when my life was filled with stress. I did nothing more than survive in this environment. I saw no relief from my misery. There were times when I wondered why I even bothered. Life wasn't what I thought it would be.

Once I realized that many of the things that were happening to me were nothing more than a test, I was able to fight my way out of them. Each experience, negative or positive, allowed me a chance to learn. The harder the test, the more I grew.

During this period, I began to notice the signs my guides were sending me, things I probably missed the first time they sent them to me.

My Story

2013 wasn't a good year for me. During that year, my house went into foreclosure, I was forced to file for bankruptcy and then my job was moved to another state. It could have been a devastating time for me, but I chose to look at it differently.

My mortgage was truly weighing me down. The housing market had plummeted since I purchased my house and it was worth less than half of what I still owed on it.

When the bank decided to tack on my town taxes, my monthly payment increased by $400. I was barely making ends meet. There was no way I could afford the additional increase. I called the mortgage company and begged them to find another way, but they were resolute in their decision.

Just let it go. Those words flitted through my mind as though they came from another person.

I sat down and thought about it. If I let it go, I'd have a period of discomfort. I'd have to swallow my pride in a very big way, but I would eventually get out of it.

When I lost my job just four months after I declared bankruptcy, I realized what was happening. My guides were removing obstacles for me. This wasn't something bad that was happening to me. It was a blessing in disguise.

I could have dove deeply into depression and allowed that to encompass my life, fully and deeply, but I didn't. I realized that what was happening to me was a gift. The Universe and all of my spiritual allies were clearing a path for me.

My life wasn't supposed to be the way it was. I was on the wrong path. I wasn't capable of making those huge changes, so the spirit world did it for me.

When I look back now, I can see the reasons for the things that happened very clearly. Had I stayed at my old house, which was weighing me down with financial responsibilities, I would have never ventured farther than my own town. The house was located in a run-down part of town. I was constantly being subjected to negative imagery and other people's drama. As someone with a strong creative side, I needed stimulation. I needed to see something beautiful and invigorating every day instead of the worst life had to offer. My situation was impacting my vibrational rate and was preventing me from maintaining a higher level. Through this, I was pulling in one bad thing after another. I needed a change.

It was then that I decided to make a huge move. I would move from Massachusetts back to my home state of Indiana, where my family lived and the cost of living was much lower.

I packed up all my belongings, said goodbye to the friends I'd worked so hard to find and I started anew. It was the hardest thing I've ever done, but the results have been worth it. I no longer experience stress about my bills and more opportunities to make money have been presented to me, almost as though they were served on a silver platter. My vibration sky-rocketed and I began attracting more positive influences into my life. I've never been happier since the move.

***

Others have had similar experiences.

Suzie Dennehy was a former student in my Paranormal 101 classes and provided me with more insight on how she increases her vibration to allow her better communication with her Spirit Guides.

60

Suzie Dennehy's Suggestions

I try and do things to increase my vibe, which includes eating plenty of veggies, doing yoga and getting enough sleep. There are times I can tolerate meat but I do notice a dip in my vibe even if I have a single glass of wine or eat a hamburger. Other things that help me are: movement, dancing, breathing exercises, anything that reduces stress, reducing coffee and sugar. If someone is particularly annoying, I use an upside down glass visualization to cocoon myself or them. To ground in order to prevent psychic vampires, I like to call on Archangel Michael to cut drama cords, and I do the white light and tree trunks growing into the earth to ground as well. I do self-reiki and sift my energy field, transmuting that energy so it is released responsibly. I've done color meditations that correspond to chakras, visualizing techniques, psychic protection and defense. Praying, releasing worries to God and trusting that I'm in good hands.

***

My friend David Rambo has several suggestions, as well.

David's Suggestions

For myself, daily meditation and pretty much an ongoing daily dialog with God, the angels and saints help me. And if you find yourself having trouble, ask them and they will help.

A vegetarian diet helps many spiritually too. Health of body is directly related to health of spirit. Practice present moment awareness. Just noticing that you have not noticed the present moment is a sign that the awareness is growing. An interesting practice the Cherokee used to teach their children was to just sit in nature and try to notice every detail about everything that they could. This helped the Cherokee with survival skills but also helps present moment awareness. And also, as the Buddhists stress, learn compassion. The electro-magnetic signal from the heart is more powerful than that of the brain. I forget the actual numbers for comparison, but compassion is a quick and effective way to connect spiritually. Art and music connect many people because it stimulates the right intuitive brain, which is half of your brain power. Very significant.

***

As both Suzie and David pointed out, diet is important for your spiritual development too.

Diet and a Vegan Life

I'm not a Vegan. I should state that up front, but I do try to limit my intake of meat, mostly due to my love of animals. After watching the very compelling documentary *Forks Over Knives*, directed by Lee Fulkerson, I came to an understanding that what I put inside my body had a bigger impact than what I first considered.

For two weeks after watching the video, I attempted a vegan diet. I removed all meat and animal products from my diet. During this process, my spirituality soared. My development as an intuitive sky-rocketed and my insight into the world of spirituality seemed to magnify. I felt better and actually lost some weight. The only reason I stopped was because it impacted meals with my son, who wasn't as keen on the vegan diet. One day, I might attempt to return to this life style. For now, I limit my meat intake.

Dana Boadway Masson has several methods that help her raise her vibration and stay better grounded.

Dana's Suggestions

Following my bliss grounds me. I like spending time doing quiet things that I have a passion for, particularly things that I need to really focus on. A couple of examples are practicing my guitar, and creating pysanky eggs (Ukrainian egg decorating - it's very intricate), or even as simple as sitting in front of the fireplace with a fuzzy blanky and a good book.

Adding fire really seems to help - I light candles when I'm doing all of the above. Candles are actually an active part of the pysanky process as well. Activities that focus my energy and make me draw inward, and use my intuition are ones that ground me.

Also, finding a spot in nature where I can sit and drink it in. I love all kinds of birds, so sitting on my back porch and watching the birds at my feeders, all times of year, is something that grounds me (it helps that I'm surrounded by forest). We also have a little stream in the back that sounds lovely when it's running in the spring. Spending some time looking up at the stars on a clear night, watching the moon over a lake... the energy of natural spaces is very healing and grounding.

***

Daniel Beaulieu often retreats to nature to raise his vibration and ground himself.

Daniel's Suggestions

I ground by going to a place I enjoy, which happens to be not far from where I live. It's a cove near the bay. It's peaceful, calming. I will walk there or drop by in my car, just get out and walk the beach or along the grassy area. I take my shoes off, breathe the fresh air, feel the earth below me, and just thank God, my guides and archangels for filling me with peace and protection.

***

For Kelly Goodrich, the key is water.

Kelly's Suggestions

Water is the most grounding proven tool I've personally come across. To sit by a pond, creek, river, lake or ocean is the best way for me to cleanse, recharge and continue with my path. The second most proven way is Earth, like a deep woods or a quiet place untouched by man and other energetic influences.

***

Once you've gotten your vibration raised and you feel grounded, it's important to keep it that way. The best method for doing this is to constantly make an effort and change your life, as best as possible, to allow positive energies to flow freely through your life.

Sometimes the changes aren't easy to make. It involves making major life changes that many of us aren't prepared to deal with. In making these changes, we will see a period of time when our vibration goes lower than it was before, but we have to do this in order to get to where we need to be. Let go of those anchors that are weighing you down so you can float to the top.

Until this is possible, another method of protecting yourself involves fortifying your space with a wall of energy. We call this shielding.

Shielding

Shielding is the practice of creating a bubble of protective energy around you to safeguard you from negative energy. While there are many ways to do this, I found the following method to be effective.

Imagine an energy ball forming at your solar plexus, your upper abdomen near the diaphragm.

Pull it up and around you like a bubble and fill it with white light. I do this every day, asking for it to protect me for 24 hours. If you don't time it, the shield will only last for several hours.

Other methods of shielding

Instead of a bubble of light, build your shield with mirrors that reflect the negative emotions back towards the sender. Sometimes I imagine myself surrounded by a giant disco ball. The visualization helps me hold the shield in place longer.

Another thing you might try is to imagine that your shield is coated with Teflon or sprayed with a clear slick-resistant substance (I imagine Pam cooking spray) that causes the energy to slide off.

You might also fortify your shield with protective stones such as black tourmaline, onyx, tiger's eye. I place them at all four corners of my house to create a physical spiritual barrier and sometimes carry them in my pocket for extra protection.

This might seem like it's taking the concept one step too far, but it genuinely works. Give it a shot and see if it's helpful.

Chakras

Another obstacle you might encounter deals with the energy centers of your body. When we talk about making a full circuit, allowing the energy to course through us fully, we need to also look at what's going on inside our bodies.

When I first began studying the metaphysical world, chakras were the hardest theory for me to grasp onto. I am a skeptic, first and foremost. It might be hard to believe, but I am one of those people who needs to see something before I believe it. I will go to the ends of the earth to disprove something before I will believe it. Ten years ago, I would have stopped reading this book at the chapter on belief.

Somewhere along the way, I decided to open my mind and at least try some of these things I heard about. I will admit to going into it while clawing onto the edges of the door. I didn't just take the information and run with it. I gave it a healthy dose of scrutiny before I allowed it into my life. Once I began studying it, I found certain aspects that truly resonated with me, so I'm asking you to do the same. Try it and see if it helps before you discount it as rubbish.

There are seven chakras in the human body. Considered energy centers, they help you move energy through your body, keeping you physically and spiritually fit. A blocked or closed chakra can prevent you from properly grounding and shielding, as well as stop you from receiving information.

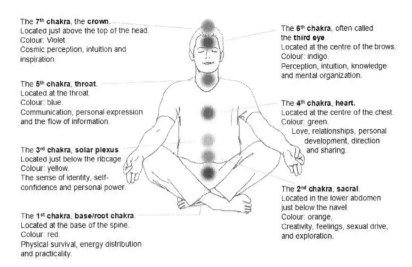

The 7th chakra, the crown.
Located just above the top of the head.
Colour: Violet
Cosmic perception, intuition and inspiration.

The 5th chakra, throat.
Located at the throat.
Colour: blue.
Communication, personal expression and the flow of information.

The 3rd chakra, solar plexus.
Located just below the ribcage
Colour: yellow.
The sense of identity, self-confidence and personal power.

The 1st chakra, base/root chakra.
Located at the base of the spine.
Colour: red.
Physical survival, energy distribution and practicality.

The 6th chakra, often called the third eye.
Located at the centre of the brows.
Colour: indigo.
Perception, intuition, knowledge and mental organization.

The 4th chakra, heart.
Located at the centre of the chest.
Colour: green.
Love, relationships, personal development, direction and sharing.

The 2nd chakra, sacral.
Located in the lower abdomen just below the navel.
Colour: orange,
Creativity, feelings, sexual drive, and exploration.

The chakras are supposed to spin clockwise and should be fully opened. When they're all spinning at the right speed, in the right direction, energy flows easier through your body. You will find that this fluctuates during the day, depending on your situation.

How do Chakras Become Blocked?

One of the primal defense mechanisms in the human mind is to mentally remove ourselves from a painful event or situation. Past hurt, pain, emotional distress and even physical health can affect our chakras. Someone who has experienced repeated rejection might close off the heart chakra to prevent more heartache. Someone with a fear of change might close down the third eye chakra.

While it's easier said than done, allowing ourselves to let go of these past hurts helps us become the people we are meant to be. Holding onto them only keeps us in the moment of the pain.

How to Open Blocked Chakras

Release the reason for the blockage. Forgive and forget. Allow yourself to understand that pain and suffering are symptoms of learning new lessons. Absorb them, but don't consume them.

When we think about forgiving someone, we have to realize that we aren't letting them off the hook easy. We are simply not allowing the poison to hurt us. We are letting it go.

Michele Lovec uses Reiki Masters to help her balance her chakras. Reiki is the practice of directing energy and is done by people who have been trained in the practice. "It's a wonderful experience if you've never tried it before. It gets me balanced when I can't rebalance myself. It gives me a euphoric feeling for days," she said.

Another way of keeping your chakras open is by keeping our bodies healthy and strong. This involves doing the things we all know we should do but often avoid. It's much easier to sit on the couch and eat potato chips than it is to go take a walk and eat a balanced meal. Sometimes it takes real effort to reach our goals.

Visualization Exercises

Visualization Exercises are also helpful for opening blocked chakras and for grounding and shielding. I've found through my years of study that visualization is key to making many things happen. There has always been a part of me that resists the concept, so I have a harder time holding images in my head. I can't see it, so it's hard to imagine it. If this is your situation as well, I can tell you that practice makes perfect.

Start with something small and work your way up. Go to your spice rack and grab a bottle. Sit it in front of you and study it for two minutes. Now, close your eyes and see it in your head. Hold the image in place for as long as possible.

Once you feel more comfortable with the visualizations, take it a step further and use it to work on your chakras.

Go to a quiet place and put yourself into a light meditative state. Lock the door, if necessary, and put your phone on silent mode. You can put on some light music, if that helps relax you. I've found that music without lyrics works best for me. Otherwise, I find myself singing along with the song inside my head instead of working on my chakras.

As soon as you feel your mind quiet, hold your hand over each chakra, starting with the crown and visualize the spinning colors, moving clockwise. Then see the blockages being removed as you focus your energy on that spot.

Once you've finished, ground yourself with a pure steady stream of white light and then repeat as necessary.

Allowing Stillness

As you've probably noticed, one of the goals to being in tune with your spiritual allies is allowing yourself to embody stillness. The mind is a cluttered landscape, filled with floating debris. Imagine trying to navigate through all the random thoughts, incessant worries and lists of goals. I always think of it as a science fiction adventure where the hero is trying to fly through a meteor storm. If you can find a way to remove all the meteors, the passage is much easier for your guides.

The best way to remove all this clutter is to learn priorities. What really matters? Does worrying about a situation really improve it? Or, are you just creating another obstacle? If we are able to tamp down on all those incessant thoughts, we create a pathway for our guides to find us.

Actively Listening

Another factor that might impede you on connecting with your spiritual allies is your ability to listen. In order to hear your guides, you must be a good listener in all facets of your life.

When someone is speaking to you, are you truly listening? Or, are you waiting for them to stop talking so you can talk? I think we're all guilty of this at one time or another. You get so excited about the topic at hand and you can't wait to share your input.

In some ways, it's a matter of utilizing patience. This is another tremendous key in learning how to connect with your guides.

Every person who is put in your path was placed there for a reason. When conversing with another person, really listen to what they have to say. Be patient and tamp down on the urge to insert your words into their dialogue. Your spiritual allies might have sent this person to you for a purpose and you might learn something.

Actively listening goes beyond the typical conversations though. It also involves simply listening to the sounds surrounding you. Stop reading for a moment and just listen to the sounds around you.

In my case, the refrigerator behind me is making a calming humming sound and a clock in the other room is ticking softly. If I listen beyond those immediate sounds, I can hear the wind gust against my house, which is followed by the sound of a car zipping by on the street.

I often participate in active listening because it forces me to connect with the here and now - the present. I am not inside my own head, solving all the world's problems. I am not making a grocery list or worrying about how I'm going to pay my bills next month. I am here. Now.

When you learn how to tune out all that conscious clutter, you are able to force yourself to be present. This place, the quiet spot between all the other sounds, is where your guides and spiritual allies will find you.

Take a few moments in your everyday life and just actively listen. As you're listening, you might also begin utilizing your other senses. What do you see while you're listening? Can you connect the sounds you're hearing to the images you're seeing? The process is very grounding, as well. Practice it as often as possible.

Turning off the "I Can't" Button

Probably the biggest obstacle you will face in connecting with your spirits is your own skepticism and lack of faith in your abilities.

It's one I faced early on too. I was interested in connecting with my own Spirit Guides after hearing about other people's amazing experiences. I wanted to try it too, but every book I read on the subject included incredible experiences.

The gifted people who wrote the books talked about interacting with their Spirit Guides as though they were physical beings, sitting right in front of them. The information was theirs for the taking. All they had to do was ask.

My experience was a bit less stellar. I sat there, and then I sat there some more before I finally gave up. In some ways, I think I was expecting my guides to walk into the room and sit down in front of me, so I abandoned the notion fairly quickly.

It took me several years to really grasp the concept and develop these methods of connecting with spirit. The first thing I did was to suspend disbelief.

Suspend Disbelief

I know you've done it before. You're watching a really good movie that suddenly takes a strange turn. You might think to yourself, "Those things don't happen in real life."

If it's a good movie, you might put your doubts aside to see what happens next. You simply go with the flow of what you're experiencing. That is what you need to do in this case too.

Forget for a moment that you haven't connected with your guides before. Forget all those failed attempts. Allow in the thought that it might be possible. It might take more time than you've given it. Another possibility is: you might have actually had contact, but dismissed the signs as imagination.

For some people, they need to experience it firsthand before they can latch onto the concept. As I've stated previously, I am one of those people.

I've been connecting to Spirit all my life, but I misconstrued this information as imagination or common sense. One time that really stands out to me came just after my divorce.

I hadn't been in the dating world for twenty years. If truth be told, I had never really dated. I met my soon-to-be husband when I was 18 years old and was with him until I was in my forties.

Several years after my divorce, two men came into my life and expressed an interest in me. I wasn't sure how to navigate these waters. I worked with both men, in some capacity. I was concerned that I needed to pick one. I couldn't imagine becoming interested in both of them at the same time. I wasn't sure what to do.

One day as I was driving, I mused aloud, "What should I do?"

An answer came to me immediately. "Neither man will end up in your life."

I gasped because the thought definitely wasn't my own. I wouldn't have manufactured that answer. If it was me, I would have probably picked one of the two.

As time passed, the voice was correct. Neither man ended up in my life. If I was looking for validation, it came to me in that moment. From that point on, I began to pay more attention to the messages I was receiving.

One thing that bears mentioning is to not overthink things.

Overthinking Your Life

I have a friend who has a hard time making decisions. As someone who is often impulsive when it comes to making choices, I find this notion inconceivable. "Just pick one!" I want to tell her.

There are times when we are uncertain about our choices. Some people will halt their entire spiritual growth by hanging on one problem. When this happens, why not reach out to your guides for assistance?

Ask the question and listen for the answer. Once you hear it, let it guide you in the direction it wants to take you. Don't second guess it. Don't let it hamper your progress.

If it's the wrong decision, so what? Move onto something else and let it serve as a lesson. If it's the right direction, you'll soon know because everything will begin to fall into place.

It might start out with making a very hard decision, like mine did when I decided to move to Indiana, but if it's the right choice, everything will swiftly begin to fall into place. This is a sign that you are on the right path.

Ask your guides for reassurance. Ask them to provide you with signs that you're doing the right thing and then listen and watch for them.

After you've removed many of the obstacles, it's time to learn how to connect with your spiritual allies.

Connecting with Your Spiritual Allies

When people think about connecting with their Spirit Guides, reality is far different from what they imagine.

If you're expecting your Spirit Guide to walk up and introduce himself, dismiss that thought. It's probably not going to happen that way. The signs you'll see will often be far more subtle, especially in the beginning.

Most of you won't be able to tell your guides apart. You won't know their names with absolute clarity and you won't see them in your head when they communicate with you. That's okay.

Your guides don't care what you call them, how you see them or if you can tell them apart. That's not why they're here. They're here to help you with your life's goals and to guide you throughout your life.

As you connect with them, you will learn to feel how they're present and hear their messages. This will happen over a period of time, something that will involve effort on your part, more than likely.

When I first decided to connect with my Spirit Guides, I read a lot of books and watched a lot of videos. In most of these, the teacher was a highly gifted individual, one of those people who easily connects with Spirit. For them, the process was easy. That's not the case with most of us.

Practice Makes Perfect

Like anything else, don't expect to master this the first time you try it. Developing a smooth dialogue with your spiritual allies takes time and effort. If your first experience is insightful and visual, consider yourself lucky. Most people will have to work hard to reach their goals, but the effort is worth it.

One friend, who I'll call Timothy, reached out to me. "If they talk to me, I don't hear them," he told me.

In his eyes, he was probably looking for a prevalent experience.

"Your guides come to you in many ways," I told him. "Have you ever just gotten a strong feeling about something and went with your gut?" I asked.

He thought for a moment and then something lit up in his eyes. "Yeah, as a matter of fact, it did. A few months ago, I was thinking about changing jobs. I had a good offer fall into my lap, but something about it didn't seem right. I couldn't come up with any real reasons, but it just didn't feel right," he told me. "I ended up passing on the new job and just stayed where I was. A few weeks later, I ran into someone who once worked for them and he told me it was the worst job he'd ever had."

At the time, he brushed the experience off as coincidence, or possibly intuition. What he didn't realize was that he was being provided with guidance from the other side. The fact that he listened to this nudge led him away from an experience that would have left him in a bad situation. Following his gut instincts was a learning lesson in itself. It gave him an example of how his guides help him.

Guides often work in mysterious ways. They send us what we need, when we need it.

Synchronicities

Sometimes our Spirit Guides provide us with opportunities that lead us to a situation that we need to experience. We have this happen to us every day, but often don't connect the dots. If you begin to employ the thought that everything happens for a reason, you'll begin to see the synchronicities that your guides have created for you.

Crystal Pina felt as though there was something missing in her life. She was drawn to the world of spirituality, but had never pursued it on her own. One day when she was scrolling through Facebook, an advertisement caught her attention. It was a flyer for a spiritual fair that was being held in a nearby town.

Normally, she wouldn't have gone to something like this, but she felt a strong nudge to attend. Once she got there, she met several people who told her about a great spirituality class they were attending and offered her a free pass to check it out. As it turns out, the class was the Paranormal 101 class I was teaching and we went on to share many positive experiences that furthered her studies into the metaphysical world.

Our spiritual allies often know what we need before we're aware that we need it. They will provide us with situations and experiences to help further our growth. Too often, we dismiss these synchronicities as coincidence.

If you pay attention to the synchronicities that are presented to you on a daily basis, you'll get a clearer understanding of where you're supposed to go and what you're supposed to do.

As I sat down this morning with the intention to work on my book, I found myself pulled into the ever additive lure of social media. Instead of putting words onto the blank page, I scrolled through my news feed, reading mindless posts about people I didn't know.

"You should really be working," a voice said inside my head.

I ignored it and kept on scrolling.

"You need to work on your book," the voice said again.

I scrolled some more.

Then, without pause, my internet connection was severed. Was this just a strange coincidence or a stronger nudge from my Spirit Guides? Who knows for certain, but it effectively pried me away from social media.

Another synchronicity happened to me several years ago, one that led me to meet someone who would become a major influence in my spiritual development.

I was invited to drive up to Maine to investigate at an old seminary. At the time, I didn't even know what a seminary was. I thought it had something to do with a church. I had no idea it was actually a prep school for kids.

I really wanted to go, but money was tight. Even though it was only going to cost twenty dollars for the overnight investigation, which was a steal when compared to the price I normally paid for that type of event, I was flat broke.

My mortgage payment was coming up and I needed to go food shopping. I told the friend who invited me that I'd have to pass on the invitation. Twenty dollars would cover half my grocery expenses and I really needed to put my money in the right places.

The following day, another friend stopped by out of the blue and handed me a twenty dollar bill. "Here's the money I owed you," she said.

I'd forgotten all about the loan. We had been out shopping and she found something she really wanted, but was short twenty dollars. I had the money in my wallet, so I loaned it to her. Weeks went by, followed by months. I'd long forgotten about the loan until she stopped by with the money.

I've been a student of synchronicity for some time, paying close attention to the Domino Effect of events that fall into my lap and following them where they go. My guides know this, so they provided me with one they knew I couldn't resist.

I called my other friend and told her I could go.

When I arrived at the event that weekend, I was introduced to Barbara Williams. I was told that she was a very talented psychic medium who oversaw the seminary building.

Over the course of the evening, I got to know Barbara better and learned about her astounding talents as a psychic medium. She has provided me with much of my foundation as a medium myself and has been a consultant on many of my books. Without her insight, I wouldn't have progressed as rapidly in my own spiritual awakening.

Placing People in Your Life

Your Spirit Guides will often provide you with connections that help advance your progress as a spiritual soul. As in my example above, my guides gave me access to Barbara Williams, who came into my life at exactly the time I needed her.

In another example, when I was first thinking about self-publishing my first book, I knew nothing about how to create a cover for my book.

I asked my guides for assistance and soon met a man who introduced me to a program called Gimp2. It is similar to Photoshop, but is a free download. Since then, I've used it on every one of my book covers.

Another person who was placed in my path happened soon after I moved to the town of New Harmony, Indiana. I was introduced to a man named Jason. It was a casual meeting at a local auction house. There were over a hundred people there and I was introduced to dozens of them. Nothing about this meeting should have stood out to me, considering how many people I met that day, but it did. I felt a strange nudge, a feeling that I needed to get to know this one specific person better.

I followed the nudge and sent him a friend request on Facebook. We began chatting and became fast friends. I still didn't understand the nudge, but the synchronicities weren't something I could ignore.

In 2015, I wrote the *Winter Woods Trilogy*. It was a suspense thriller set in a fictionalized version of New Harmony and followed a twin girl named Winter. Imagine my surprise when Jason told me that he had twin daughters and one of them was named Winter. What were the odds of that? Before I wrote my books, I'd never heard of a person being named Winter, but here was a real live version in the same town my book was set in.

After hearing this, I knew I was being led somewhere. Over the course of the next few months, Jason and I became closer friends. He took it upon himself to introduce me to many people in town, people who would eventually share their stories with me for my upcoming book about the town's haunted history. He also introduced me to his friend Denise, who is a caterer in town. After getting to know her, I began teaching a monthly painting class at her catering shop, which helped me bring in more money and meet more people.

Much of this I can attribute to what I call nudges.

Nudges

Our Spirit Guides come to us in different manners. Some people actually see and hear them, while others have to play a spiritual game of charades with them. Even though I've gotten to a point where I can catch the occasional message, most of my insight comes from being nudged in a certain direction.

Have you ever gotten a strong feeling that you need to do something? It's sort of a nagging feeling in your head that won't let go until you've fallen through with the task. I call these nudges.

I get them all the time. In fact, I had another one recently.

Because of my new friendships, the local newspaper heard about my endeavors and wanted to write an article about me. Once the article was published, several people in the local area reached out to me. One of these was Crystal Folz, who is a psychic medium. I was stunned to hear that she was also the manager for a Halloween prop and costume company called Gore Galore.

I knew this was going to be an important connection because this was the second time Gore Galore came to my attention. In October, my new friend Jason had invited me to attend a presentation that was being held at the famously haunted Willard Library in Evansville, Indiana. The owner of Gore Galore was giving a talk about how they make Halloween props and costumes. It was a great presentation and we were both intrigued by all the gory props. I didn't think anything of it until Gore Galore popped back up on my radar.

Crystal and I met for coffee and hit it off right away, promising to get together again soon. Several weeks passed and I meant to get back in touch with her, but never thought about it at the right time. Then I got another nudge. I needed to get my hair cut.

When I thought about the haircut, an old friend came to mind. I had gone to high school with Cheryl Edwards and kept in touch with her on Facebook from time to time. Every time I thought about getting a haircut, her face popped up in my mind, so I finally made an appointment.

I was happy I did. Not only did I get a great haircut, but afterwards as we were standing in the lobby, Cheryl asked me if I'd met any new paranormal friends since moving back to Indiana. I immediately told her about Crystal.

"She works at Gore Galore. It's a company that makes these amazing Halloween props. Have you heard of them?" I asked her.

Cheryl pointed over my shoulder. I turned to look and saw a man walking up the sidewalk. "My next client works there," she said.

I was floored. Gore Galore is a small company that probably employs somewhere around a dozen employees in a town that is at least twenty miles from the salon. What were the odds of that?

I took it as a sign that I was supposed to reconnect with Crystal.

I contacted her that very day and set up another coffee date. We soon became great friends. She's been instrumental in helping me unravel some of the hauntings in my new town, which helps me research my upcoming *Haunted New Harmony* book. I'm sure there will be more to this story that will unwind over time, but it showed me the importance of paying attention to the things that happen.

By following that initial nudge, I allowed the dominoes to tip over, one after another until they led me to the place I was supposed to be. The connections will definitely help me with my goals and I'm thankful to my guides for providing them to me.

Psychic Medium Brandie Wells also guides her clients to listen to the nudges. "What are you being nudged to do?" she often asks. "What are you being asked to do? We all have the ability to listen, we just don't pay attention. I think it's fascinating that people think their thoughts are their own, but they're really not. You are influenced by divine universal force, every day, all day. Your thoughts are not your own. It is your connection to your Higher Self and everybody has that," she said.

During one of our coffee dates, Psychic Medium Crystal Folz told me about a few of her nudges.

"I get them all the time," she told me. "Sometimes, I'll jump in my car to drive to the post office, which is only a block away, and I'll forget to put on my seatbelt. Then, it will come to me that I need to put on my seat belt. I'll put it on, then turn the corner and see a cop sitting there," she said.

While being prevented from getting a traffic violation is important, she's had more prevalent times when nudges have helped her.

"I think it's very important when we follow those nudges. That's when I really started to grow in what I do was when I started listening to those," she said.

A week before she was scheduled to do a reading for someone, she kept seeing two strange images in her head. "I kept seeing this tree that was suffocating. I could feel it. It felt like that tree had been on fire or something was burning in front of it. It was driving me insane. I would drive and would think about that tree. I'd go to bed and think about that tree. It went on for a week. Then, I started thinking about a tricycle that was missing a foot pedal. It would stay in my head and it would go on and on. I couldn't get the tricycle with the missing foot pedal out of my head," she said.

"It was a random thought. I don't have little kids, so it doesn't make any sense why I would be thinking about it," she said. A week later, she learned the reasons for the two images.

"I went to my house reading and when I got there, I saw a tree that had been burned. They had burned a shed in front of it and the tree caught on fire. One whole side of it was charred black. When I walked up onto their porch, I saw a tricycle with a missing foot pedal. Those things let me know I was in the right place," she said.

The case ended up being an important one that involved children. Crystal's assistance was pivotal in the family's recovery from a tragic event that left negative energy in the space, creating a toxic environment for the family. The nudges she received helped her understand the importance of her involvement in the case.

Like Crystal, listening to the nudges has greatly impacted my development as a medium. Because my guides know that I am receptive to this form of communication, they use it frequently to get my attention. For other people, the prompts might present themselves differently, depending on what they react to.

Meditation

Hand's down, meditation is the fastest way to connect with your Spirit Guides and spiritual allies. If you already practice meditation, this won't be difficult for you, but if you're like me, it's like asking a wind-up toy to stop moving mid-jump.

I've never been one who can sit in one place for very long. Even while I'm writing, I find myself easing out of my chair to go change a load of laundry or check social media to see what's going on in the world. The concept of sitting down for a half hour, doing nothing, is difficult at best.

My recommendation is to start small.

Five-minute Sessions

Find a quiet place where you won't be disturbed. Put your cell phone on silent mode. If you can manage it, dedicate this time slot to spirit guide communication. For example, you might decide that Friday mornings are good for you, so plan your weekly communication for every Friday at 10am. If you have more time to spare, do this daily instead of weekly.

Once you get your time and location established, follow the list below:

1. **Create a sacred space.** You want to be safe and secure in this space while you open yourself up. Some people like to burn sage or incense beforehand to raise the vibration of the area and remove negative pockets of energy. Other people will often say a prayer, asking for their higher power or Spirit Guides to keep them safe during their session.

2. **Ground and shield yourself.** Pull protective white light down into your body and release all the energy that does not serve you. After you feel grounded, pull that white light into a protective bubble around you. Only energy from the light will be able to reach you inside your shield.

3. **Get comfortable.** I recommend sitting down, as opposed to lying down, for the session. If you are too comfortable, you might inadvertently fall asleep. Make sure the clothes you are wearing aren't too tight and won't distract you. The room should be a comfortable temperature, at least in the beginning. As you continue with meditation, you will find that you can get into the zone much faster and that distractions won't inhibit you.

4. **Close your eyes.** Focus on the colors that come through your eyelids. Some people will leave a light on, so they can see this as they meditate.

5. **Focus on your breathing.** Take one deep breath in and hold it for three seconds, then exhale. With every breath, imagine your body relaxing. Start with your feet. Imagine

them becoming weightless, and then move up to your legs. By the time you get to your head, you should feel the muscles in your neck start to relax.

6. **Clear your mind.** If a thought comes to you, release it. Just continue to pay attention to your breathing and the light you can see through your eyelids.

7. **Ask for your guides to come to you.** Do this in your mind. They can hear you telepathically. You don't need to speak the words aloud, in this case. Ask them a simple question and see what comes into your mind. The first response is usually the answer. Once you start analyzing it, you might second guess the response. Don't. The first response is the right one.

8. **Close the session.** As the five minute mark approaches, close out the session. Thank your Spirit Guides for coming to you, whether you felt them or not, and state aloud that you are ending the session, but invite them to communicate with you any time.

As you get more comfortable with this, you can increase the five minute time span. Start slow and build your way up. Move up to a ten minute time span for a while before you go to fifteen minutes.

Some people prefer to use guided meditations. You can either find someone who leads meditation groups or you can find guided meditations online. I've used many of them and have found them to be helpful. Try a few and see what you think. What works for one person won't always work for everyone.

Psychic Medium Brandie Wells also uses meditation to help her connect with her Spirit Guides.

Brandie's Story

"I did a guided meditation to meet all of my guides, not just my Spirit Guides, but all the guides who work with me. I was absolutely shocked. I had Jesus float up on my left side and Mother Mary with her eyes half opened float up on my right side. I'm not a religious person. I do believe in God, but I believe in many gods. My belief is that if it's through love and light, it's of the highest good. It doesn't matter to me what your belief system is. I have tapped into past lives and have a lot of past life guides still working with me which is why I'm so open. I've tapped into many different elements of my Spirit Guides," she told me.

***

Another method I often employ involves passive meditation.

Passive Meditation

Have you ever found yourself zoning out while you're in the midst of mindless activities? You might find yourself daydreaming or simply allowing your mind to wander while you're washing dishes, driving long distances or mowing the grass. This is a form of meditation. I call it passive meditating.

Sometimes we need to occupy the body in order to relax the mind. By doing something physical that doesn't require much mental involvement, we are allowing our minds to reach a place where we can better connect with our guides.

My friend Sandy finds herself in this place when she works in her garden. Having your hands in the earth is a very grounding experience to begin with. It gives her solace and a sense of tranquility that allows her to go deeper in her mind and communicate with her Spirit Guides.

When I find myself in this place, I often reach out to my guides. I will ask them a simple question in my mind. It might be as simple as "Am I on the right path?" which only requires a yes or no answer. Or it could be more involved, like, "What could I be doing differently to better myself?"

The trick is to listen and believe the words you hear after you've asked the question.

Another method for communicating with your guides is the simplest method. Simply ask for help.

Prayer

Prayer comes in many forms. It doesn't have to be the standard method. Sometimes it happens during odd moments of the day when you need to grasp onto your faith for comfort and guidance. Many people use prayer to connect with a higher power, which includes our Spirit Guides.

Jeff Torgalski uses prayer to make the connection. "I usually pray to my Spirit Guides to come to me before bed or use my magick ash candles to summon them," he said.

Dreams

Frequently, our guides will come to us when we are sleeping. Our conscious minds are cluttered with thoughts and images, but our sleeping minds are far quieter. Many people have reported having dream visitations from passed on loved ones, as well as from their guides.

A true dream visitation will seem far more vivid than a normal dream. It will be the dream that sticks with you when you wake up because it feels more like a memory than a dream.

Often, the messages come as symbols to us. Other times, the message is clear and easy to interpret.

If you get a symbol, think about what this means to you. If my guide gave me a red rose, I would think about one of my grandmothers who loved red roses. If your guide gave you a red rose, it would have a different association for you. Think about the symbol and try to determine what the meaning is for you.

My friend Jill Anne had a dream visitation that she shared with me.

Jill's Story

I had a dream one night almost one year after my father passed. Even more ironically, it was two years exactly to the date that my mom passed.

In the dream, I was finishing up a sexual assault case at Lawrence General Hospital when they declared an emergency status because of a large accident that occurred. They asked me for help because they were shorthanded. For some reason, my daughter was with me, which is something I've never understood or figured out. We were helping a woman and her two children whose husband/father was not doing well and the medical team was coding him.

While my daughter and I were helping them, my father and a man were suddenly standing there together surrounded by light as if the sun was shining behind them. I look at my father exasperated and asked, "What are you doing here?"

"Everything's complete," he said with a huge smile on his face, which was strange because my father rarely smiled.

I just looked at him confused and said, "What?"

Again, he said, "Everything's complete." Then, he and the man faded away and I woke up.

Up until that point I had received a number of signs I believe were sent by my father through songs, smells and encounters. After that dream I haven't received anything I felt was from him. To me, I feel he's "passed on" and gone onto whatever his next step was to be. Whether it's a new life or some other experience, I believe that's where he is. I always have very vivid dreams. Even when I dream about my parents, he's always very much in the background and we don't engage with each other. I only engage with my mom.

***

In Jill's case, her father returned to act as a family guide, to provide her with guidance in her waking life. The dream was a symbol for a real life situation she was encountering. It simply took some deciphering for her to understand that her father was telling her that everything was okay.

Tima Amaro has had several signs from her brother Jose, who passed away at the age of 45.

Tima's Story

I left my family in Florida to be with my brother until he took his last breath. I was called in a dream before I came to Massachusetts. I stayed in the same room with him for a week with him on one bed and me in another. I didn't eat or sleep for that entire week.

After he passed, I went back to Florida. I had a dream that first night that I was up in the clouds looking for him, worried and calling out his name.

He appeared to me in the clouds and was oh so handsome. I ran to him and we hugged. He was no longer sick. He said the nickname he had for me (Fatocas) and asked, "Why are you worried and wondering where I am? You helped get up here, you know I'm with Jesus!"

For his funeral, I got to pick out the card with his picture and saying on it. It was a picture of clouds with Jesus hugging a man, like welcoming him to heaven. I just thought it was appropriate because I had to get my brother to ask God for forgiveness before he died. He had a hard time but finally did at the end.

One week later, my family and I went to my cousin's house in Peabody because they looked after him while he was sick. It was the first time I had been to this house.

I walked into the house and the first thing I saw was the exact picture that I picked out for my brothers funeral. It was an 8x10 in a frame on the wall.

My heart dropped and of course I cried! I asked where she got that and she said it was my brothers and that was his favorite picture!

My cousin said she bugged when she saw this picture at the funeral but didn't tell anyone that she had the same one at her home.

I miss him so much!

After his passing, Tima felt compelled to look at the sky and saw his image in the clouds.

***

Shannon DeLap also feels her Spirit Guides in her dreams, often when she's faced with a difficult decision. She will dream about them giving her sound advice. One of her more relevant encounters came when she was thinking about moving to another state. "It was almost like a lucid dream, but my guide told me it was time to move forward. He said that nothing good would come from staying." The move ended up being a good experience for Shannon and she's thankful for the input.

My friend Elizabeth "Lizzie" Leonard, who is the owner of Terrapin Traders in Gardner, Massachusetts, where I taught my Paranormal 101 classes, shared a personal story with me about her son.

Lizzie experienced something that no parent should ever endure. She lost both of her daughters early in their lives. Her daughter Renee died in 2006 and her daughter Brenda died in 2007. The impact was tremendous for the entire family, but hit her son Michael especially hard.

After going through a bad situation, Michael tried to harm himself. He shared this story with his mother, who shared it with me.

Michael's Story

I felt lost, alone and defeated. I went to bed that night and this is my dream. I woke up to voices of kids playing. I sat up and tried to shake off the sleep. When I looked up, I saw Brenda and Renee sitting on the floor, playing with dolls. I thought I was hallucinating. After rubbing my eyes, I looked again and my nine and ten year old sisters were still there, playing on the floor.

I sat there for a minute, just watching. Finally, I slid a little closer. To make sure they weren't playing with my mind, I called to them by their names. Without looking up from their dolls, they said, "hi."

I asked them what they were doing here. They said they were playing with dolls and asked me if I wanted to play. I told them that I didn't play with dolls.

Brenda got up and hugged me. I remember crying. Renee appeared by Brenda's side. I told her how much I missed her. She said they had to go. I begged them to not leave.

Renee turned and smiled and said, "We never left you. We'll always be by your side."

I woke up crying and so happy. Although I still get sad sometimes, I've never wanted to hurt myself again.

***

Lizzie said the experience really changed Michael. It made him realize how much he has to live for and how his sisters are still there for him. She's proud of the fact that they came to him and saved him.

They have appeared to him many times since to comfort him.

"Renee was very protective of Michael, even though he was older than she was," Lizzie said. At one point, Michael asked why they kept coming to see him. Renee seemed perturbed by the question. "Why do you always ask that? You know you always wake up when you ask that," she told him.

Lizzie told him to keep paper and pencil by the bed so he could write it down when it happens.

Lizzie and I spent a few minutes talking about the encounter. Her biggest question was why both of her daughters, who passed away as adults, came back to Michael as children. I turned the question back around to her. "Why do you think they came back as children?" I asked. Her response made sense to me.

"I think they came as children because it would remind Michael of happier times of them together. I think they were trying to take him back to another time when things were easier. I always encouraged them to enjoy their childhood and not be so concerned about growing up," Lizzie told me.

I thought it was a beautiful story and was thankful she shared it with me.

***

Marna Wright had several dream visitations that proved pivotal during a difficult time in her life too.

Marna's Story

"I've had dream conversations that I've never forgotten with who I can only describe as very wise people during critical periods of my life," she said.

After years of having difficulties adding to their family, she underwent In Vitro Fertilization (IVF) procedures seventeen years ago. "This caused me stress because, although we had two healthy twins, I felt guilty. I would have loved more children, but my husband shut down every time I initiated a conversation. As far as he was concerned we had 2 healthy babies and we should not press our luck," she said.

She couldn't stop thinking about those 17 frozen embryos. She thought about adopting them out, but couldn't do it. She even considered just letting them thaw out, but the thought was inconceivable to her.

"Now that I had met their siblings they were my real potential children," she said. "We were in between a rock and a hard place and Stephen really would not budge. In fact, he would get more upset with every conversation."

"One night, when my twins were two, I had a dream I was talking to someone very wise and kind and female. She was both young and old at the same time. I don't recall what she looked like. I don't think she was quite human but she looked human. I asked her what I was going to do about the embryos. She told me I should try to have another baby. I told her that my husband would never agree to it. She said, 'This weekend, he will agree." I woke up excited, like I knew a special secret. I felt that way all day. The next day, which was Saturday, an opening came for us to discuss the embryos again. He simply said, "This is clearly something you need to do. Do it.'"

"We had a frozen embryo IVF procedure done. I was pregnant for about 2 weeks only. I was very sad but also grateful because to this day I think someone who "knew me," stepped in and helped me resolve an impossible situation. We never did IVF again and still have 2 children.

For Marna, it wasn't a Hollywood ending, but she couldn't fully describe the peace that she felt about the entire situation.

"I think she came because of the guilt and stress that the situation was causing me. You can't believe the choices you have to make when you want children so badly but your body won't go along," she said.

In this case, her guides were there to comfort her and help nudge her towards making a decision, something that had weighed heavily on her mind for years.

***

My friend Dana Boadway Masson had an especially helpful dream visitation that helped her get through a potentially terrifying experience, as well.

Dana's Story

When I was in early pregnancy with my son, about 7 weeks along, I started having what I was sure was a miscarriage. I called my clinic to see if they could book me in for an ultrasound the next morning. I was certain it would just confirm my worst fears. I had a hard time sleeping that night, but eventually I did.

I had a dream that night...

I was in a big ballroom that was packed with people, milling around. At the very far end of the room, a set of double doors opened up, and I saw my grandpa walk in (he had passed about 4 years prior). He made his way towards me through the crowd, and when he got close to me, I could see that he was a young, strong version of himself, and he was sooooooo happy. He reached out, and gave me the BIGGEST hug. He was ecstatic. When I woke up, I knew he was telling me that everything was ok.

Sure enough, I went to the clinic, and the ultrasound tech found my son's heartbeat right away, and it was strong and steady.

And my son is now almost 5 years old, and boy, does he ever remind me of my grandpa.

***

Author Gare Allen shared a dream experience in his book *The Dead*.

Gare's Story (as told in *The Dead*)

That night, I dreamt of my mother (who had recently passed away). We were sitting on a front porch step and she was telling

92

me that she was going to be reborn as a girl in Greensboro, North Carolina. After our chat, she said she had to leave. I watched her drive down a highway, and I feared for her safety on the busy roads. In the dream, I had a birds-eye view of the interstate and to the right of her car, I saw the same vast field with the colorful trees, running dogs and trail that I had seen in my own dream and during my visit to Greensboro.

I woke, knowing that my mother was going to be alright.

In this, and countless other dreams of my mother, she would never look at me. Her eyes would either be blurred out or she would not be facing me.

At first, I took this as concerning symbolism but then I recalled a phone call we received just hours after my mother passed. She had signed up to be an organ donor and they wanted permission to remove her eyes.

Once I remembered this, I would see her eyes in my dreams.

***

Gare's story shows that love holds no boundaries and that death only separates us physically. Our loved ones remain with us, providing us comfort and guidance.

Kelly Simmons also had information come to her in a dream.

Kelly's Story

I have always been intuitive since I was a little girl. When I was six months pregnant with my first son, I had a psychic dream about my aunt, who I was very close to. But due to bickering between my mom and aunt, I hadn't seen her in five years.

I very vividly dreamed of floating above my aunt and following her to a hospital to see a doctor. I saw her getting tested, including a CAT scan, and saw the doctor giving her bad news that she had cancer. I then envisioned fast-forwarding to her funeral.

I told all of my family that morning, especially my mother. It was so vivid and detailed; I knew something had to be wrong with her. I begged my Mom to call her or her husband, my uncle, to check on her, but she didn't call her right away. She was trying to work up the nerve. The next evening, my uncle called my mom and told her that my aunt had Stage 4 brain cancer. She passed away less than a year later.

This is just one of my many experiences where spirit intervened and showed or told me things I couldn't have known. It was quite a profound and sad moment in my life, but I realize that my Guides and crossed over loved ones were letting me know. They wanted me to know, that no matter what, she'll be okay and with me especially, since I was pregnant. I feel her around me a lot and it gave my mom and I a chance to reconnect with my aunt and tell her we loved her and to say goodbye.

***

Kelly's story was very poignant and essential in helping her ease the pain of grief. My guides have also helped me in my dreams.

When I was considering moving to Indiana, I was appropriately nervous. Packing up and moving a thousand miles away was a daunting idea. What if I didn't like it there? What if things didn't work out?

I had a dream one night that put everything in perspective for me. In the dream, I saw myself sitting on my front porch enjoying a sunset. My new neighbors came over to welcome me to town and I felt a sense of euphoria, knowing I made the right decision in moving.

Because I seldom remember my dreams, this was an important moment for me. I woke up feeling optimistic about the move and immediately began making plans.

Soon after I made the move, I found myself sitting on my front porch, feeling content and happy with my decision as my new neighbors came over to welcome me to town. My guides knew I needed this clarity, so they provided it to me.

Asking for Assistance

This might seem like a no-brainer and it is. Most of the time, our guides won't interfere with our lives unless we invite them in. I say "most of the time" because sometimes they do come to us when we don't ask for it. Unfortunately, we often miss the signs and dismiss it as coincidence.

Ask them to provide you with signs that will have meaning to you. If you're like me and pay attention to synchronicities, ask them to place people or situations in your path to help you navigate.

Leslie Kim Herrington-Matilainen, who is a Holistic Psychotherapist, Reiki Master and Harmonic Sound Therapist, often asks her guides for signs. "I hear them talk in my mind, come to me in dreams or receive symbols when I ask for them such as feathers or dimes," she said. She once had an interesting experience where her guides came through to provide her with life altering information.

Leslie's Story

For four years, Leslie searched real estate listings, looking for the perfect property, one that was meant for her.

"I was feeling impatient and so I asked my guides," she said.

She then heard the sound of waterfalls. She didn't understand what it meant, but tucked the thought aside, knowing that it would pop back up if it was important.

The next day, a home came up on the real estate site. In the pictures, it showed waterfalls coming out of the back of the house. She bought the house soon after and has never been happier.

"Later, I attended a workshop for Akashic Records. We got to ask a question, so I asked why I was meant to have water falls. I was taken on a bird flight around the globe & shown that all the water ways are connected," she said.

Leslie uses gongs and singing bowls in her healing practice and has discovered that her new house is perfectly suited for her gifts.

"When I play gongs and bowls and send healing intention, the energy runs down the outhouse hole (which I painted and removed the seat to hear the falls while on table). The energy flows down and out so it can heal the planet," she said.

"Others have told me it is a sacred Ley Line spot where native spirits stand watch. Visitors often see the spirits in my backyard on the river. The falls flow to an underground brook that comes out at the back of my home as an above-ground brook and then flows to the back of my yard into the river," she told me.

"My clients cannot believe the powerful energy in the healing room. I often see the same animal spirits they see when they're on the table while I work on them. I always invite their guides and mine to assist," she said.

***

Author Gare Allen shared this encounter in his book *The Dead*.

Gare's Story (as told in *The Dead*)
My mother had grown up near the water and often told me of the days that she would enjoy driving along the beaches with the convertible top down on her car.

During my childhood, we made frequent trips to the beach. Her favorite water spot was Ft. DeSoto Beach, which is where I spread her ashes.

I recall the drive to Ft. Desoto Beach after her memorial. I asked Selene (Gare's spirit guide) for a pod of dolphins as a way of honoring my mother. I was more than grateful to see that when my brothers and I spread her ashes into the ocean, not one, but two pods of dolphins swam and jumped through the waves, just yards from us.

***

Other Animal Signs
In a recent gallery reading, Psychic Medium Brandie Wells had a woman who kept seeing butterflies and wondered if it was a sign.

Once Brandie tapped into her energy, she received the message, loud and clear. "When you see a butterfly, think of me," the voice said. Brandie feels that our loved ones often send animals as messengers.

"Animals are on the same vibrational frequency as humans. That's why, as humans, we can connect with animals. Different animals hold different meanings. For example, the other day I was doing a reading for someone and a blue jay came through."

Brandie thought this was interesting because blue jays often symbolize how people use their power and their voice. She felt it was very representative of someone who was loud and wanted to be heard. When she told her client about this, the client instantly knew who it was.

"The cardinal is a classic," Brandie went onto say. "The cardinal is sent a lot because it's so bold and easy to be seen. We are so oblivious. As humans, we don't realize that everything goes beyond synchronicity. It is all being aligned for us at every single moment. Nothing is by accident. They try to pick the boldest things that will catch your attention. The cardinal is one of the most common things they will send."

I thought this was fascinating information. When I wrote my book, Signs of Spirits – When Loved Ones Visit, I reached out to people on Facebook and asked for their stories. Many of the stories regarding birds were about cardinals. I didn't understand why so many people were seeing the same breed of bird, which made Brandie's story truly hit home for me.

Here is one of the stories I shared in my book.

Maria's Story (as told in *Signs of Spirits – When Loved Ones Visit)*

Maria De Fatima also had an experience with cardinals. She had been close with her father, who had always loved cardinals. After he died, she began seeing a single red cardinal in a pear tree outside her house.

She walked outside with her camera and spoke to the bird.

"Dad, if that's you, then you will let me take a picture and you won't fly away," she said, calmly approaching the bird. The bird allowed her to get within touching distance without even fluttering a feather. He sat still until she took the picture and then flew off into the distance.

***

Butterflies are also used frequently by our loved ones and Spirit Guides to pass on messages.

Kristen's Story (as told in Signs of Spirits – When Loved Ones Visit)

For Kristin, the sign was butterflies. Her mother's death hit her hard and was difficult for her to handle. When she got married several years later, thoughts of her mother accompanied her throughout the day. She wished her mother could have been there with her. It didn't seem fair.

After the wedding, they released a boxful of butterflies. Most of them flew straight up into the sky, happy for their freedom, but two of them stuck around. They kept landing on her and wouldn't leave. In her heart, she knew it was her mother and her grandmother, who had also passed away, letting her know that they did attend the wedding and were there to share in her joy.

***

Sometimes our guides are with us, providing us with clues that we don't always notice. Numbers are one of them.

Paying Attention to Numbers

One of my friends is a fan of numerology. He watches the numbers that come into his life and uses those to help him with decisions. One day, he saw a license plate with several fives in it, got a receipt for lunch that totaled $5.55 and kept finding himself looking at his watch when the time had several fives in it.

He looked the meaning up online and learned that seeing fives often means that a change is coming. The more fives you see, the bigger the change. As it turned out, the sign was correct. Shortly after he began seeing fives, he was offered a new job at a different company and his entire life changed soon afterwards.

For me, the number signs were twos, but I didn't understand the message.

When I first started writing, I thought that writing the book was the hardest part. I was expecting fame and fortune to swiftly follow, which obviously wasn't the case. I sent my first completed manuscript off to several agents and then waited for the responses.

As time went on, the responses came in. Some of them were outright rejections, while others asked for changes. My entire life revolved around my mailbox.

During this process, we moved to a new house. The address to the house was 232. When I went to open a post office box, I was given box 22. I got my first cell phone and the number included four two's. Even our landline phone number contained many two's. What did this mean?

While I noticed them and pondered over them, I didn't understand the message. This was years before the internet became so accessible, so I couldn't just log on and research it. Later, I learned that seeing twos means that your guides are with you and are aware of your aspirations, but are telling you to be patient. Some dreams take a while to manifest.

Shortly after my experience with the numbers, my guides sent me one more sign.

The book I was working on involved a character and her dog Fugly. Fugly was a terrier mix who was so ugly, he was almost cute. I described him as being approximately forty pounds, with long grey hair and a severe under bite that left him with a face only a mother could love.

While I was waiting to hear back from the agent who was reading my book, I worked part-time at a local pizza shop. The work was grueling and hot, as we worked in front of a hot pizza oven in a building that didn't have air conditioning. One night as I was working, I looked up to see a dog standing in the open doorway.

My jaw dropped. The dog looked exactly like Fugly, down to the unattractive under bite.

I dropped the pizza dough I was working on and sort of drifted to the doorway. As I got closer, I realized the dog had been recently sprayed by a skunk. For most people, this would have been a tremendous deterrent, but not for me.

I was currently working on a sequel to my Fugly book and had just written a chapter about him getting sprayed by a skunk. My mind raced as I stood there, looking at him. Could this be Fugly?

I ended up bringing him home with me that night. He didn't have a collar or dog tags, so I had no idea where he came from. I gave him a much needed bath and removed most of the horrid skunk smell and set him up in my home office with a comfortable bed, toys and food.

Much to my dismay, my husband suggested that I post flyers to see if I could find out who he belonged to. I grudgingly followed his instruction and received a phone call several days later. Someone owned the dog.

The woman came out to pick him up and was delighted to be reunited with him. The minute he saw her, he left my arms and raced to where she stood and showered her with kisses.

As she turned to leave, a thought occurred to me.

"What is his name?" I asked, praying she'd say Fugly. Instead, she said something that rocked me to the core.

"His name is Destiny," she told me.

In that moment, I knew that I was following the right path. It was my destiny. I didn't end up getting that first book published. In fact, I wrote five more before publishing my first book, which was actually my seventh completed novel. I've written sixteen more since then, so my patience was worth the effort.

Since I didn't understand the reason behind all the twos, my guides provided me with more clarity by giving me a direct message.

A Basic Guide to Numbers

If you are curious about what a specific sequence of numbers might mean, I'd suggest going online and typing them into your search engine. Here are the basics:

Seeing Ones – People often see the time 11:11 and attribute it with making wishes. The truth isn't too far off the concept. When you see a series of ones, it means that your guides are there for you and that you should pay attention to what is going on around you. When I see ones, I always take it as a good sign. I begin paying attention to what is going on in my life and look for synchronicities or nudges.

Seeing Twos – As I stated in the example, this means that your guides are present, trying to make things happen for you. Be patient while you're waiting, because sometimes the blessings might take longer to manifest than you'd like.

Seeing Threes – If you see a series of threes, it could be a sign from your guides to pay better attention to what is going on around you. They are trying to get your attention to a blessing that has been sent to you.

Seeing Fours – Fours are a sign from your guides that they are there with you, helping you. Fours also suggest a need to find courage to push through difficult obstacles, knowing you are being fully supported from the other side.

Seeing Fives – Fives mean change is coming. It could be a good change or a bad change, it depends on the situation. Even bad changes can be beneficial for us because they teach us valuable lessons. Just brace yourself and be prepared.

Seeing Sixes – If you suddenly begin seeing a lot of sixes, it could mean that you need to seek better balance in your life. Have you been working too hard or focusing on something that consumes much of your energy? It might be time for a breather.

Seeing Sevens – People often talk about seven being a lucky number. In Angel Numbers, this is the case, as well. Seeing a series of sevens means that you are on the right track and should keep pushing forward.

Seeing Eights – Eights are mostly about abundance. When you see them repeatedly, it could mean that it's time to look at your finances. It could also mean that abundance is on its way due to your hard work and diligence.

Seeing Nines – Seeing nines is often a sign that endings are on their way. It might be time to take a look at your life and take an inventory. Is there something in your life that no longer serves you? It might be time to let it go.

Numerology and Angel Numbers are intricate and often difficult to interpret. Take note of the number and look it up online. If something happens that corresponds with the message you received, then document it for future reference. I see them all the time, now that I pay attention to them. They don't always mean what I think they're supposed to mean, so it's taken me some time to figure it all out. Sometimes the message will be different for you than it might be for someone else.

After going through a week-long period of seeing frequent 11:11s on my clock, I took it as a sign to ask my guides for assistance on something I was working on. Not long afterwards, the answers began coming to me as though Heaven-sent.

There are times when I have difficulty interpreting the messages though. My mind is too cluttered with thoughts for me to reach a spiritual plane where I can hear them clearly and the numbers don't make sense to me. When this happens, I reach for my pendulum.

Pendulums

The art of using a pendulum dates back hundreds of years. People have used them for a variety of methods. You don't have to go out and purchase something expensive. A pendulum is anything that

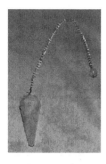

hangs from a string and has the capacity to move when held. When I can't find my pendulum, I often grab a necklace.

As with any divination tool, I always create a sacred space to work with my pendulum. I set the intention that I am only willing to communicate with my spiritual allies or my Higher Self before I begin.

Psychic Medium Brandie Wells also uses divination. "I use my pendulum or dowsing rods to make sure that my connection is clear between myself and my Spirit Guides," she said.

Here's an excerpt about pendulums from my book *Dark and Scary Things – A Sensitive's Guide to the Paranormal World.*

Setting the Energy on Your Pendulum

If it's the first time you've used a specific pendulum, you will need to align your energy with the pendulum. To do this, hold the pendulum steady with one hand and put your other hand below it.

Once you've aligned your energy with the pendulum, you don't need to always hold your other hand beneath it. Steady your elbow so you aren't inadvertently moving it.

Hold it steady and ask for what "yes" looks like. The pendulum will begin swinging either back and forth, side by side, or in a circle. This is what "yes" looks like. Now, ask again for what "no" looks like, as well as "maybe" or "I don't know."

How to Use a Pendulum

The biggest trick to using a pendulum is learning how to keep your hand steady so you don't affect the outcome. Even the smallest movement can cause the pendulum to swing in a certain direction. For the best results, try resting your elbow on a table.

Tips:

- Start off with basic questions.
- Ask "yes" or "no" questions unless you want the pendulum to point to a specific direction, such as "where are you in the room?"
- For more specific responses, use a chart with letters of the alphabet, asking Spirit to spell out answers.
- Stop when your arm grows tired. If you don't, your responses won't be as valid.

Charts

A chart can be hand-drawn or printed, as long as it's legible and provides enough room for the pendulum to swing. Always keep in mind that the pendulum swings back and forth, so the chart should be a half circle.

On the following page are two basic charts. You can find many others online, but I prefer to keep it as simple as possible.

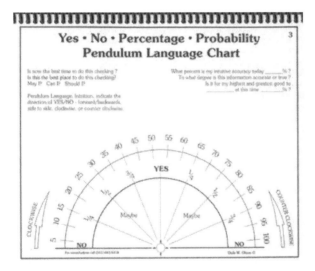

This chart can provide you with basic "yes, no, or maybe" responses, along with a probability range, while the chart below can provide you with more clarity.

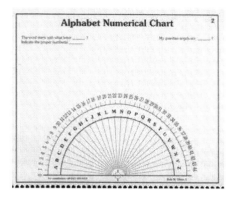

Another divination tool you might use to connect with your guides involves using dowsing rods.

Dowsing Rods

Dowsing has been employed for centuries, especially when used to find water beneath the ground. Old-school diviners typically use a forked branch, although modern methods vary.

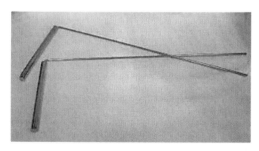

Modern dowsing rods consist of two L-shaped rods, made of copper or other metal. Many home-made varieties are shaped from old coat-hangers. For best results, the handles should have a sleeve to allow the rods to move freely.

Dowsing can be used for a variety of functions. You can use them traditionally, to locate underground water, or you can use them to find lost items, hidden graves, or to communicate with Spirit.

Method: As with any divination tool, ground and shield yourself before you begin. Then, hold the rods steady, making sure they don't move on their own. Slight hand movements will cause the

105

rods to react, so holding your hands very steady is key to getting real responses.

Like with a pendulum, ask for what "yes" looks like. Then, ask what "no" looks like. The rods will either open or close, depending on the preferred response.

Ideomotor Effect

Skeptics are quick to dismiss the use of pendulums or dowsing rods because of our propensity to affect the outcome. Subtle movements can change the way the pendulum swings. I have no problem with this.

One way to determine if you are impacting your responses is to look at the answers themselves. If you are connecting with your guides or spiritual allies, you will often get responses you weren't expecting. I once felt a new spirit come into my space and began asking a series of "yes" and "no" questions. I even threw a few test questions into the mix that I knew the answer to.

I started by attempting to narrow down the options by asking if it was one of my grandmothers. The pendulum said yes. I then went through the names of my grandmothers, fully expecting one of them to say yes, but it didn't. It kept telling me no.

I was uncertain at this point, so I asked a test question. "Are you my Aunt Martha?" The pendulum responded with yes. I sat back, dismayed by the response. I didn't have an Aunt Martha. Why was it telling me yes?

It was then that I remembered my step-mother's mother. Her name was Martha. Armed with this information, I asked, "Are you Grandma Cross?" The pendulum began swinging immediately in the yes response. This confirmed to me that I was making contact and wasn't inadvertently yielding the response I was expecting.

Another consideration is the fact that you might be connecting to your Higher Self. If you are making a small movement to affect the outcome, doesn't this mean you already know the answer?

You might be tapping into your Higher Self, which is just as good as connecting with your guides.

As you try all these methods, keep track of your progress. Start a Spiritual Journal.

Keep a Spiritual Journal

Your journal doesn't have to be fancy. It could be leather bound or a spiral notebook you picked up at the drug store. All that really matters is that you use it.

Every time you experience something that feels spiritual in nature, jot it down. Make a note of the date and time this happened, as well as the situation you were experiencing when you felt it. It will help you begin to see the patterns.

For me, I might jot down that last night at 7pm, I had the urge to turn off the television and start painting. Since moving to Indiana and removing most of the stress factors from my life, I've returned back to my creative roots and started painting again. The process has been very spiritual for me, as well as financially lucrative. People have been inquiring about purchasing my works of art, which led me to teach a painting class.

I followed the nudge and returned to my painting. An hour after I started, I received a message from a friend, asking if I'd paint a picture of her daughter's pets.

The next night, I received the same nudge again at 8pm. This is normally the time that I spend relaxing and binge watching Netflix. I began to see a pattern.

After thinking about it, I realized that my guides were prompting me at times when I was the most relaxed. They knew that I would have a better chance of producing something beautiful when my mind and body were in harmony.

When I paint or write, I often feel as though I'm not doing it alone. While I'd like to think that it's all coming from me, I know better. There are times when I get into my zone and just allow the spirit to move through me, guiding my hands, either on the keyboard or by holding a paintbrush. I will type words that I don't grasp the meaning of and will employ techniques that I've never considered before. This is when I know my guides are with me.

Talented photographer Phil Koch also feels his guides when he creates his beautiful photographs. "The spirit guides me to each and every Horizon showing me the light and the simple grace of the natural landscape," he said. Phil has been a Facebook friend of mine for years. The images he produces have a very spiritual aura about them. The tranquility and sense of peace in them speaks volumes of a higher power at work.

Brian Kent also feels his Spirit Guides through nudges. He describes them as primarily thoughts that make sense. They often come to him as logical advice that he often follows, knowing the source might be from his deceased father. "It's a daily occurrence. Yesterday, I had a stop on Hwy 66. Something influenced me to go around a certain farm ahead of me, so I turned. I went around the farm and came back around from another direction and saw a farmer herding three stray cows across the road. It saved me from being held up and FedEx drivers don't like to be held up," he told me.

Despite what you've experienced, you might be surprised at the various ways you'll feel your guides.

How You Might Experience Your Spirit Guides

Everyone feels their guides differently. For Psychic Medium Barbara Williams, her guides simply stepped in and helped her during her first encounter with them.

Barbara's Story

Barbara was born with many metaphysical gifts, but that didn't mean she automatically had all the answers. They came to her gradually with every lesson.

She knew she was different from the other children. She was able to connect to spirits and ghosts from an early age, but she hadn't yet learned how to talk to her guides. That too would come in time.

Her first encounter with her Spirit Guides came when she was thirteen-years-old, living in Pennsylvania with her family.

She would sometimes sneak out at night. She'd tell her parents she was going to the library, but would meet her boyfriend at a nearby playground.

"The playground had a big metal gate and it was always open. It was so huge, you could ride on it and swing it open," she said. After they spent some time hanging out at the playground, her boyfriend suggested they go for a walk on the road outside the playground.

As they started down the road, her heart was light and she was simply enjoying the evening. She was caught up in the moment and didn't feel anything foreboding, but when they passed the open gate to the playground, she couldn't go any further.

"It was as though there was a giant rubber band across the road and I couldn't go any further," she said. "I had no words to express what was happening. I was fumbling around, not knowing what to say to him," she said.

No matter how hard she tried, she simply couldn't break the invisible barrier that stretched across the road. She tried to walk away and then walk back through, but something wouldn't allow her to go any further. After the third attempt, she just gave up. She told her boyfriend that she didn't want to go for a walk after all and suggested they return to the playground.

The next day, an article appeared in the newspaper that brought some clarity to the situation. A young couple was murdered in the exact spot where they were planning to walk to. If she and her boyfriend had arrived there first, they would have been killed instead. Someone was definitely looking out for her.

It was then that she connected the dots. "Oh, that's why you didn't want me to go there," she thought, her mind spinning with the implications. It really hit home for her and was confirmation she would utilize for the rest of her life. "I knew from that point that I was being guided," she said.

Barbara's husband Steve has learned to connect with his Spirit Guides over time, as well. Sometimes, when he's driving, his guides will tell him when police are nearby, so he can slow down and avoid a speeding ticket.

His progress with his guides wasn't always easy though. A few years ago, he was getting frustrated that he couldn't see his guides. He asked Barbara if she would help him. He wanted to know if her guides would tell his guides that he wanted to see them up close and personal. Seconds after asking, he saw a giant Native American face pop up in front of him. It was shocking to him, but was the confirmation he needed.

Other times, Spirit Guides help out in more prominent ways. Kathryn Bertolino shared a story with me where a family guide stepped in and assisted.

Kathryn's Story

I have a wonderful story about my grandfather coming back just a few days ago to help my grandmother. My grandmother just turned 90 and has had a couple of falls over the last several months. Another fall would be a disaster. So my grandmother moved in with my parents and my little sister.

They had a cat named Scotty who was very sensitive. During the storm last week, Scotty's heart couldn't handle the noise and he died while everyone was asleep. He passed away in the hallway between my parent's room, my grandmother's room and the bathroom.

Shortly afterwards, the power went out. My father got up to get a flashlight. When he stepped into the hall, he tripped over the cat. If that had been my grandmother she would have broken bones.

I believe my grandfather, who passed decades ago, shut off the power, then woke up my father.

***

Psychic Medium Crystal Folz shared a story with me about the first time she met her family guides.

Crystal's Story

I had my first really profound experience when I went through my first Reiki attunement. During our meditation, I saw all of these women in front of me. They were different ages, different races and different clothing. I had my eyes closed, but I could feel them and see them in my mind's eye. It was a whole overwhelming feeling of "we're all right there with you." That really sealed that universal connection for me. I could feel all of these women. All of their DNA is in my DNA. All of their thoughts and memories are in me. I just need to tap into that.

I've always felt that my guides are feminine, because they all feel very strong, nurturing and empathetic."

Crystal reads the energy that surrounds living people and can often pass on messages from deceased loved ones. Like many of the psychic mediums I interviewed, she has a difficult time determining where the information is coming from.

"Sometimes it's hard to decipher. I don't feel like I've ever connected with a 200 year old Native American who's telling me where to go and what to do. I just know. It's always just been such a part of me.

She does often pick up on deceased family members though.

"I pick up on my husband's aunt and my grandmother and I just know they're right there with me during certain times, when I need something. It's not the sense that someone is there, guiding me through my life. It's more that there are people who step in and give me support when I need it," she said.

"One time, my husband was playing a gig in Madisonville, Kentucky. Before he left, I said, 'You should have one of the guys follow you home,' but he blew me off.

"All night, I sat and worried until he finally called me at 12:30. He had narrowly escaped hitting two dogs, but in doing so, he ran off the road and blew out two tires. The guy I wanted him to have follow him was long gone. There was no one behind him to know that he'd almost been in a horrible accident, so he had to wait for them to come back to help him," she said.

Even though Crystal doesn't always know who the nudges come from, this time she was fairly certain it was his aunt who was sending the message.

Her story struck a chord with me because my grandmother has been with me for most of my life, helping me out in similar ways. When I was nineteen years-old, she popped into my head and told me to slow down, preventing me from rolling my car when my front tire blew out.

***

Others have reported similar encounters, but the following story is unique, because Psychic Medium Brandie Wells learned this information secondhand.

Brandie's Story

I think my most amazing experience was not my own.

When my daughter, who is twenty now, was five years-old, she really opened me. I've been an animal communicator my whole life. As a child I could feel and hear and know what animals needed and wanted. When animals were injured, they would come to me. I didn't realize my other abilities until my daughter opened me.

She was five years old. She came running out of her room after I tucked her in that night. She said, "Mommy, Mommy. This noise just came to me. It was a sparkling boy and a big white wing brushed my face and it tickled!"

I thought, "Okay." She's a very factual child, not a child with a vivid imagination who would make up stories. I told her, "If you ever have something like that happen again, I want to hear about it."

Between the ages of five to eight, I documented everything that she told me and it is profound. I'll give you a quick overview of what I learned from my daughter.

You only learn lessons while you're here on this earth's plane. You can't learn lessons in any other place. You can't learn them when you're in Heaven. You can't learn them in any other realm. That is why we're here.

We're here to learn lessons through the deaths of our loved ones, through the birth of a child, through every experience you are learning. You are experiencing that for your soul, your spirit, to learn.

It was mind blowing for me because it gave me a perspective about why we're here. I used to think, "Why would someone come in with a disability? Why would God do that to someone?" The reality is: it's their journey. You have to honor their journey in this lifetime. What are they learning from that? If you look at everything as a learning experience and not get so hung up on the emotions, it's much clearer. You need to zoom out and look at the big picture and realize that everything is teaching us a lesson. It's all about the growth of your spirit.

I know I was meant to hear this, because later on when I opened my spiritual self, I saw all of this.

One of the final things I've really carried with me is that when we die, we leave an impression on a heavenly realm. We are energy and we are able to split and divide, but we can never dissipate. You leave that impression on the heavenly realm so that all who have loved you, can still stay connected to you. Because you are energy and can split and divide, that's where old souls come from. Your energy continues to move on and into new beings. That's where the growth and the journey of the spirit is. All of us are able to continue to connect our energy cords. Those cords of energy between us and those we love stay connected even when we die. That's how we can still hang onto a piece of them.

My experience through Spirit Guides is really the energy cords of my daughter, who has opened me. It opened me to see the world in a different way. It taught me to honor all people. No matter who you are or where you come from. I don't care if you're a murderer or you're a priest. There is a reason why you're having that experience and it's not just for you. It's for everyone else who experiences you, as well. There's a reason for all of this. It's just fascinating to me. Now, I look at each individual and honor their journey, no matter where they come from. There's a purpose. It taught me to honor the purpose. I may not like some of the choices people make, but there's a reason why it's being presented. It creates that balance of the darkness and the light, the yin and the yang. Without the darkness, there wouldn't be light and without the light, there wouldn't be darkness.

I also believe we pick our own parents. One of my daughter's first sentences was "Mommy, I picked you." She described what it was like to be in the womb. She said, "It was dark and warm but I could hear your voice and I picked you."

***

My friend and fellow author Gare Allen's first encounter with his spirit guide Selene was documented in his best-selling book *The Dead*.

Gare's Story (As told in *The Dead*)

During my very first attempt (at astral projection) I fell asleep during the relaxation process and then woke as I was lifting out. I floated up and my perspective was the surroundings of my bedroom. While I could plainly see my physical form sleeping on my bed, I could not see my *astral* body. Although I felt them, I was unable to see my hands or legs so I don't know what I was wearing or even if I still looked like me.

When I realized that I was "out", I thought, immediately, that I wanted to go to the moon. After a whirling sound around me, I felt a surge of rapid movement and then I was there.

Walking beside me on the lunar surface, as if completely normal, was a beautiful, dark haired woman. She boasted impossibly high cheek bones and large, dark, loving and knowing eyes. The angelic creature stood inside a glow of soft, white light. She seemed pleased at my presence and briefly described to me the art of astral travel.

"On the astral plane, your thoughts instantly create. Focus is necessary to maintain your location."

I felt a sense of achievement as we walked. Looking down from the surface of the moon to Earth, I could see a long, silver cord stretching from somewhere on my backside.

The woman explained its purpose. "It will remain tied to your body and connected until your physical death."

I then asked her name and I received this response, "I am your spirit guide, your protector and family. My name is Selene."

Gare's first introduction was the first of many encounters he would have with Selene.

***

Spirit Guide, Deceased Loved One or a Ghost?

Some of the signs are often similar. Deceased loved ones acting as guides might exhibit some of the same signs you'd experience from a ghost.

In my book *Signs of Spirits – When Loved Ones Visit,* I talk at length about the ways you might feel a deceased loved one. Some of the stories are truly amazing. Here's one example:

Paula's Story (as told in *Signs of Spirits – When Loved Ones Visit*)
I have experienced so many of the examples on this list that it is uncanny. One of my favorites being one that happened two days after my mom had passed.

I was busy getting the funeral arrangements finalized so I was out and about early with a long morning of errands. All I could think about was having my (current) favorite sandwich for lunch - very specifically, a turkey with mustard and Swiss cheese on a bulky roll. Very odd that such a thought would be running through my head at that time, and I definitely had none of the ingredients on hand.

I got home, arms full of things, mind on overdrive, only to be met by an old friend and long-ago neighbor. This was someone who had been close to our family, but we had not seen much of in recent years. She had been thinking of me and wanted to drop off lunch. The sandwich she handed me was "as ordered" right down to the bulky roll. I knew immediately it was a sign from my mom that all would be well.

***

Some people might scoff at some of the stories and say that they're just coincidence. As far as we know, some of it could be random scenarios playing out in a way that causes us to analyze them, but many of them aren't.

Spirits reach out to us in any way they can. It must be quite difficult for them to garner our attention. Imagine trying to wield your way through someone's cluttered thoughts to pass along a message. Often times, the message will be denied because the person receiving it doesn't believe it to be true.

When people come to me with their visitation stories, I always ask them, "What was the first thing you thought about when you received the message?" In the example above, Paula immediately thought about her mother. The thought was linked to the action, which gives it far more relevance. If she didn't connect the dots, then it probably wouldn't have been a message. Her mother made sure that the situation came with the thought of her, almost like putting a name label on a carefully wrapped gift.

You Will Feel Family Guides Differently than You Feel Spirit Guides

Spirit Guides work in different ways than deceased loved ones who are helping you. Your Spirit Guides have been with you since your first incarnation and will be with you throughout all your lifetimes. They usually connect with you on a deeper level. They speak to your soul.

Deceased loved ones have a closer connection to their former world. They might have received divine instruction after passing through the light to Heaven, but they still fall back on gestures they once did when they were human. They might touch you when you're feeling sad or leave keepsakes for you to find. You might find a penny on your doorstep or a feather on your pillow. Or, you might feel a touch on your shoulder, similar to the way your loved one might have comforted you when he or she was still alive.

In truth, knowing the difference between a deceased loved one and a spirit guide isn't important. Both are there to help you and you can trust their message. You should, however, know the difference between them and someone who hasn't crossed over into the light yet.

The Difference between a Deceased Loved one and a Ghost

When this happens to me, I always turn to my emotions. How did it make me feel? If I felt comforted, it was probably a family guide. If it left me fearful, it was probably a ghost.

My friend Leslie Rose reached out to me with a story that she wasn't certain about.

Leslie's Story

I once had a shadow man sitting in my truck next to me. He popped up while I was on 95 northbound. I looked over, tapped my brakes because he scared the crap out of me. He was pointing ahead.

I looked in front of the truck and saw a big piece of round metal come flying at my windshield. It cracked it but bounced off. I pulled over at the next rest stop and called the cops, afraid the chunk of metal would be on the road and dangerous to others, because it was the size of a basketball. They never found it. I didn't tell them about my visitor. It was the only time I saw a shadow person that close up. He had a hat on like the black-hatted shadow men.

***

Leslie and I had further discussions on what the shadow man might have been. She was concerned that he might have been a true shadow person, which is an entity that is usually negative in nature, but I didn't feel this was the case. While I don't think it was a spirit guide, it could have been a family member attempting to help her. Sometimes our deceased loved ones will provide us with an image that will capture our attention. Showing her a shadow would have taken much less effort than showing her a clearer image. The fact that he warned her about oncoming danger shows that he was helping her. Shadow people wouldn't do that.

If it was a ghost, he was being quite helpful. She's never seen him again, but is thankful for the intervention.

It does bring up an interesting point though. How do you tell the difference between your spiritual allies and ghosts?

One place to start is with your spiritual allies. Your Higher Self knows the difference, as do your true Spirit Guides. Each encounter will also come with a built-in emotion. It's up to you to decode it. There are several factors that might help you.

The Message Will Always Be Positive

Your Spiritual Allies, which includes your Spirit Guides and deceased loved ones, will never make you feel bad about yourself or attempt to scare you. If the message is from your guide, it will always be positive. Your guide will never tell you that you that you look fat in those jeans. Your guide will tell you that you are beautiful just the way you are or perhaps suggest an activity that might bring you to a healthier version of yourself.

They Won't Scare You

Your spiritual allies will never do something to make you shriek in terror. Their messages are always gentler. They want to guide you, not frighten you. If something jumps out and frightens you, this isn't your guide.

The Message Will Be Lighter

Typically, your guides will provide guidance in less obvious ways. If your television set continues to turn itself on and off, it's not your Spirit Guides doing it. It might be a deceased loved one, who is attempting to help you, but it won't be your true guides. They will come to you in less evasive manners, through nudges, dreams or internal thoughts that aren't your own.

The Message Will Be in the Third Person Context

You won't hear, "I'm doing the right thing." You will hear "YOU'RE doing the right thing. I use this often when I'm confused at the message. Like many of you, I often wonder if the thoughts I feel are coming from me instead of from one of my trusted allies. Thinking back to how the message was conveyed has helped me many times.

As I've stated in previous chapters, everyone feels their guides differently, depending on their level of spiritual awakening and their metaphysical abilities.

I often connect with my guides in a different manner. Because I am intuitive with some mediumistic abilities that allows me to communicate with spirits and ghosts, I am able to connect with my guides more clearly.

How to Connect with a Ghost

Ghosts linger in our plane of existence for a variety of reasons. Communicating with them is often difficult, because they haven't received the divine council they would get if they had crossed over into the light.

I always caution people about initiating contact with anyone who isn't from the light. One of the reasons for this is the margin for error or deceit. A ghost can often pretend to be someone else in order to gain your trust. If you've read any of my other books, you'll understand why this could be a problem.

Ghosts have different agendas from spirits. They are often trapped here in the physical earthly plane of existence, hoping for a resolution for their death or to pass on a message for a loved one. Some of them have darker intentions though.

I often encounter what I call "energy vampires."

It takes a tremendous amount of energy to maneuver in our world. People use food, sunlight and other natural sources to keep themselves going. Since ghosts don't have access to any of that, they have to find energy where they can. As a seasoned ghost hunter, I can tell you that I've frequently had the batteries instantly drained in especially haunted locations. The ghosts pull this energy from my batteries so they can use it for themselves.

Others bypass the batteries altogether and use your energy instead. This is called a Paranormal Hangover.

Here is an excerpt from my book *Dark and Scary Things – A Sensitive's Guide to the Paranormal World.*

Paranormal Hangovers

People who investigate the paranormal often endure what we call a Paranormal Hangover the following day or days after an investigation.

Why does this happen?

The logical assumption is that we simply didn't get enough sleep after being awake all night chasing ghosts. While this does have some relevance, and certainly has an impact on the way a person will feel on four or five hours of sleep, it doesn't explain everything.

We have to credit the ghosts themselves for some of the energy drain.

As we've discussed previously, ghosts need energy to communicate and they're going to take it wherever they can find it. I believe ghosts are like people: some figure things out much faster. Higher performing ghosts will know how to pull energy from the living, so keep this in mind when you visit a location with a heightened level of activity. The smarter the ghost, the more you're going to feel it the next day. If the ghosts are chatting with you all night long on your digital recorder or your Spirit Box, they have to get this energy from somewhere. It's not like they can go eat a box of Wheaties or plug themselves into a power outlet.

Protecting yourself is really key in these types of locations, something we'll discuss in detail in an upcoming chapter.

Recovering from a paranormal hangover is actually fairly similar to recovering from an alcohol induced hangover. Here are some tips:

- Get enough rest afterwards. If you stayed out until four in the morning and didn't get into bed until six, then it stands to reason that you will need to sleep until one or two in the afternoon. Many people just can't do this since it interferes with their internal body clocks. The best thing to do is to sleep as long as you can and then get up and make the best of it.

- Keeping yourself fully hydrated will help, as well. Even though you might crave coffee or energy drinks, stick with water until you're fully hydrated. Caffeine can act as a diuretic, causing you to dehydrate even further. Drink plenty of water.

- Get out and stay busy. When faced with a paranormal hangover, most people just want to vegetate on the sofa in front of the television set all day. While it does help kill the time, it won't help you recover. Get out and enjoy the sunshine and fresh air. You'll be amazed at how much better you feel.

- Eat a balanced diet, but load up on protein. Our bodies crave protein when we are energy depleted. Proteins, such as lean meats, nuts, and eggs can provide you with a boost to help you recover your energy.

- Stay away from refined sugars and processed, salty foods. I always crave soda and chips when I'm feeling energy depleted, but neither serves to help me regain my energy. Wholesome foods, like green leafy vegetables, fruits high in Vitamin C, and plenty of water are your best allies for regaining your energy.

- I also find that an investigation often disrupts my normal sleep pattern, leaving me off schedule for days later. I combat this by taking a melatonin supplement before bedtime on a daily basis. I've found that 5 mg works well for me, but always check with your doctor to find out the correct dosage. This will vary from person to person.

- Go to bed on time the day after an investigation. Fight the urge to nap during the day. This will only prevent you from getting to sleep later when it's your normal bedtime. Avoid watching television or using a computer for several hours prior to bedtime, as well as avoiding caffeine. Everyone is affected differently by caffeine. I've found that if I avoid it after two in the afternoon, I'm usually fine by the time I retire for bed at ten in the evening.

Communicating with ghosts is very similar with the way you would communicate with deceased loved ones or your spiritual allies. They can communicate with you telepathically, but unless you are metaphysically gifted, receiving the information can be daunting. I recommend using a digital voice recorder or a pendulum to initiate conversation. Insure that you ground and shield yourself properly before the dialogue to resist them from following you home later.

I had an interesting experience as I was writing this section about my encounter with an earthbound soul.

My new town of New Harmony, Indiana, is filled with ghosts. Considering its history, this isn't surprising. It was founded in 1816 as a Utopian Society by a group of Lutheran disciples. Religion was of the utmost importance and the rules were strict. They practiced communal living, sharing chores and responsibilities. Men and woman were required to remain celibate, even if they were married.

After ten years, the group grew weary of the isolated location and sold the town to another Utopian society. This group, known as the Owenites, focused on scientific studies and education. The churches were turned into schoolhouses and laboratories and children were removed from their homes to be educated in the country's first kindergarten system. This group lasted two years before the property was sold to the people who resided there.

When I first moved here, I was astounded by how many ghosts lingered around the town. As a sensitive, I could feel ghosts in almost every building.

One building in particular had a strong presence. As I walked into the old antiques shop, I became aware of a female lingering near the back of the store. In my mind's eye, I saw her as being a young adult, perhaps in her late teens or early twenties, with dark hair and a thin build. She was wearing a simple blue dress that made me wonder if she had been an employee from an earlier period.

Every time I visited the store, I acknowledged her in my mind, but never attempted any further communication. Yesterday was a different story.

As I walked through the store, I felt her stronger than I'd ever encountered before. It was as though she came out of the back room and ventured out to where I stood. As a Clairaudient, I hear a tone similar to buzzing or ear ringing. Each ghost has a different tone, which is how I make the initial contact. Once I hear the tone, I can pull in more information and physical details. Once again, I acknowledged her and then headed back home.

A few hours after I arrived home, I heard the same buzzing sound that I had previously heard in the antique store. Internally, I groaned, since this happens to me far too frequently.

She hovered near my bed as I tried to go to sleep.

"Please let me sleep and we can talk tomorrow," I told her.

She backed off and I enjoyed a restful night's sleep. Early the next morning, she returned, as planned.

In my former role as a paranormal investigator, I would have been intrigued by the contact and would have attempted to collect evidence of her presence. Through time and experience, I no longer feel the need to prove anything to anyone. I know she's there and my top priority has shifted to something else. I want to help her, if I can.

I spent about fifteen minutes talking aloud to her. I told her that God loves her and her family members miss her. I told her about letting go of the experiences she had when she was living and about crossing through the white light where she could find peace and happiness. I then envisioned a brilliant white light opening above me and ushered her into it. She crossed over quickly, ending nearly a century of suffering.

Using Your Spiritual Allies for Paranormal Protection

If you frequently communicate with the other side, chances are you will eventually run into a ghost that makes you feel uncomfortable. This has happened to me more times than I can count.

When I first started expanding my abilities, I hadn't yet unlocked the gift of connecting with my spiritual allies. I knew they were there, but I had no way of talking to them. As a result, dark energy often followed me home from paranormal investigations.

After meeting Shaman Michael Robishaw and witnessing the power of using Spirit Guides for paranormal protection, I began working with my guides as well.

As a sensitive, I can feel when a ghost is nearby. Someone who isn't sensitive, might feel them in one of the following ways.

How You Might Sense a Ghost

Bad Luck – Have you recently had a string of bad luck happen to you? It feels as though nothing is going right. Appliances seem to keep breaking and your cell phone keeps losing all its contacts? Tech savvy ghosts are capable of bringing bad luck to our lives.

Odd Smells – Ever smell something in your house that doesn't make sense, like the aroma of baking bread, floral perfume or cigar smoke? These are signs ghosts sometimes give us to alert us of their presence. Loved ones often use these signs as well. Always think about how the smell made you feel when you first detected it. If it made you remember your grandma, it probably wasn't a ghost.

Missing Items – Do you feel like you're always looking for misplaced items? Ghosts often play a spectral game of hide-and-seek with their living room-mates. An item will go missing, only to turn up in an unusual place. People often blame this on a lack of sleep or a busy schedule, when in fact, it has a vastly different explanation.

Frequent Nightmares – If you are plagued with frequent nightmares that have a different texture from your normal dreams, you might look deeper for the cause. Blame it on the pepperoni pizza you ate before bedtime, but it could be an entity trying to rouse you from sleep.

Exhaustion – Ghosts need energy and they often pull it from the living. Paranormal investigators frequently discover the batteries on their equipment draining at haunted locations and feel exhausted after an investigation. Ghosts will pull energy where they can find it. A typical sign that a ghost is using your energy is the sensation of vibration. When they pull energy from us, sometimes their vibrational rate is different from ours, giving us the feeling that we are vibrating from the inside out.

Strange Photos – When you upload your pictures from your camera or cell phone, do you ever find strange streaks of lights in the photos? Ghosts typically don't show up in pictures like we expect them to. Often, they appear as streaks of light or strange unexplained mists.

Odd Pet Behavior – When your cat or dog watches something moving around the room, don't immediately brush it off as being an insect. Pet's vision differs from ours, allowing them to see a broader spectrum of light. They might be seeing something paranormal that you can't see yourself.

Frequent Ear Ringing – Do your ears ring at strange times? While this could be due to a medical condition called tinnitus, it's also a mediumistic ability called clairaudience. People with this ability will often hear a tone that is similar to ear ringing. The next time it happens, turn your head to see if you can localize the sound. Is it moving around the room, growing fainter as it gets further away? If it is, chances are you're hearing a ghost.

Unexplained Nausea – Some people get physically ill when a ghost is present. The sensation is typically presented as a sudden upset stomach and the feeling you are close to vomiting. Try leaving the room and see if the feeling abates. If it does, you might be physically reacting to the presence of a ghost.

Feeling Watched – Do you ever get the feeling that someone is watching you? You turn, but don't find anyone else in the room. This is a frequent sign of a haunting. The sensation is usually unnerving, at best. Try moving from the room to see if the sensation goes away.

If you feel any of these signs, ask your spiritual allies to help you. I often light a stick of white sage and smudge my house from top to bottom, moving in a clock-wise pattern through my house. While I'm doing this, I call out to my Spirit Guides and spiritual allies and ask them to surround me with protection and to assist me in removing the unseen visitors.

Here is what I say: "I fill this home with love and light. All negative energy that is not from the light must leave. I call upon my Spirit Guides and spiritual allies to help me remove this energy."

Once I've finished, I walk out my front door, while encouraging the energy to follow the smoke. I then stub out the sage stick on my front door stoop. Afterwards, I spray all of my doors, windows and exterior walls with holy water and then create a solid circle of sea salt around the exterior of my house. This creates a sacred spiritual boundary that will help keep you safe.

It took my guides a while to master the ability to help me remove negative energy. I was a bit daunted. I reached out to Shaman Michael Robishaw for guidance. What he told me was a bit shocking. He felt that I was probably a new soul and had younger guides.

I was astounded by the information. I don't think anyone wants to hear they are a new soul who hasn't experienced many lifetimes. I wanted to be an old soul, filled with knowledge and capabilities.

The information made sense though. I began working with my guides as I cleansed my house, telling them exactly what I wanted to do. Through time and effort, they have gotten much better at helping me stay protected.

Other Signs of Spiritual Allies

There are times when our spiritual allies provide us with information in the form of tokens, mementos and strange occurrences.

As we've already discussed, some people will find things like coins or feathers in odd places. Others will have odd things happen in their lives.

After Tela Zully-Roger's father died, both she and her mother experienced flickering lights in both of their homes. "He died in 1995 and to this day our lights still flicker in our homes. I always say "hi Dad". I know it's him," she said.

For Crystal Pina, the sign was also flickering lights, but in a different manner.

Crystal's Story

Something really weird happened to me this morning. I was driving down a country road and two cars were headed towards me on the other side.

The first car started flashing his headlights at me, like when there's a cop hidden ahead, except he kept flashing me. As he got closer, I noticed that only one headlight was flashing. So I started thinking that maybe he was a cop because how could he make only one headlight flash and not the other? And why did he keep on flashing me?

I was going a tiny bit over the speed limit - maybe 5 miles over, if that. So I slow down to probably 5 miles under the speed limit until I figured out what he was trying to tell me.

As he got closer, I realized he hadn't been flashing me at all. It was the way the light was shining through the trees, every time he went past a tree it blocked the light and made it look like he had been flashing me but I was already driving slower by then.

Just as I rounded the bend, there was a cop standing in the middle of the road. He was directing traffic around a truck that was cutting tree limbs. If I hadn't slow down already, I would've had to screech on my brakes to avoid hitting him. I wouldn't have been slowed down already if I didn't think the guy was flashing me that there was a cop hidden. It was just an odd coincidence.

You know, sometimes when you drive down a country road and you just drive, not really paying attention because there's not much to look at? Because I thought he was flashing me, I was actually paying attention to what was going on around me and I was able to stop in time.

***

Julie Susalla also had an experience

Julie's Story

I was adopted by people who were abusive towards me in every way, to the point that I considered suicide at the age of sixteen. It was at that moment of time I received the message from someone in spirit that if I didn't leave, I'd end up hurting myself.

It was a thought out in my head but almost like I could hear the tone in the person sending it. I think it was my mother who passed when I was three.

I listened to Spirit and left. Whenever I get where I feel like giving up, I hear from Spirit again that everything's going to be alright. They are with me.

Another time, I was heading up to Michigan for my oldest brother's funeral. It was in June and I was in a blubbering state while I was driving. The whole right side of my car suddenly frosted over on the windshield side windows and on the rear window, front to back. In the empty passenger seat, there was a cold spot. The entire left side of the car was clear, so I could see to drive. When I noticed this oddity, I heard in my head, "I'm here sis. I will be here until you get over the mountains."

When I got over the mountain, I again heard his voice telling me "You got this now," and all of the windows cleared up and the cold spot in the passenger seat was gone. I knew it was my brother.

I've had several readings by mediums who've all said that my brothers, father and mother are always around watching over me with smiles on their faces.

How Gifted People Feel Their Guides

People with metaphysical gifts have a sixth sense they are able to utilize. Sometimes, this gift allows them a deeper insight into the invisible world that goes on around us. This includes having more transparency with their Spirit Guides.

There are many types of Sixth Senses that people might have. I will go through the more common types.

The Clairs

There are five primary methods that intuitives might connect with the spiritual world.

Clairvoyant means "clear seeing" in Latin and refers to someone who sees the spiritual world in their mind's eye. These people have the clearest ability to sense their guides because they often see them in their mind. People like Barbara Williams, who is a gifted psychic medium, sees her guides in detail when they come around.

Clairaudient means "clear hearing" in Latin. People with this ability will hear ghosts and spirits. Some hear music, while others hear voices or sounds. I hear tones that are similar to ear ringing. Over time, I've learned to differentiate between the sound a ghost makes and the sound a spiritual ally makes. Spirits have a clear bell-like tone, while ghosts sound more like static or white noise.

Some people actually hear their guides speak. Betty Johnson told me, "I hear one, just before I'm going to do something really stupid, like marry my last ex-husband. The judge asked, "Do you take this man?" My guide said, "Do you REALLY?" I did, but I regretted it and got a divorce 14 months later.

Lauren Possick often gets an overwhelming feeling of peace and unconditional love. "I sometimes get a little shaky too," she said. She also hears something she calls "harmonics." She describes it as a sound that is similar to a guitar.

Clairsentience means "clear feeling" in Latin. If you have this gift, you will often feel ghosts or spirits physically, either through touch or with physical symptoms, such as a headache, stomach clinching, goosebumps or nausea.

People with this ability are often able to touch objects and connect with the energy attached to it. This is called psychometry.

My friend Sandy is clairsentient. When she feels a ghost or spirit near her, she gets a tingling feeling on her scalp. To gain greater clarity, she has asked her Spirit Guides to always make the tingling sensation on her left side, while ghosts affect the right side.

Paula Braman-Duarte also feels her family guides physically. "When my parents come calling, I feel a gentle pressure on my left shoulder and then on my right. I place my hand up by the first pressure area and feel some gentle energy and then do the same on the other shoulder spot, completing the connection we three had in life. Mentally, I talk to them for a minute thanking them for making their comforting presence known."

Clairalience means "clear smelling" in Latin. Typically, people with these abilities will detect an odor that no one else notices. One member of my class often smells her mother's perfume when her mother visits her in spirit form.

Kelly Goodrich always gets the scent of rose perfume from her grandma, when she comes to visit. Others might detect pipe smoke or a specific food aroma.

Claircognizant means "clear knowing" in Latin. This gift allows the person insight into the spiritual world. Information simply comes to them. They often know things they shouldn't have access to. People who have this often discount the information as coincidence or imagination until they've had an experience they can't easily explain.

Empathy is the ability to feel energy and emotions, from both the living and the dead. It is thought to be connected to Clairsentience, although it often demonstrates talents from many of the other Clairs. Empaths are often overwhelmed by the surge of energy and emotions that swirl around them. Parting through the fog is often difficult and daunting. Learning how to ground and shield energy is essential for their well-being.

When an Empath feels his guides, he might experience emotions. A sudden onset of happiness might be a sign from his guides that he's on the right path. If he gets sad or angry when considering other options, this might be a sign that he should go in another direction. It's important for Empaths to listen to the emotional nudges they get, because there might be a message attached to them.

Samantha Lynn is gifted and experiences her Spirit Guides in a variety of ways.

Samantha's Story

"I am very intuitive. I'm clairvoyant, clairaudient and clairsentient. I see flashes, colors, they talk to me in dreams and feel them with me 24/7," she said.

"Earlier this year, I heard a voice say to me, 'He is the answer you seek.' I knew without a doubt my two years of chronic pain were coming to an end. Last night before drifting off to sleep, I heard my name called.

"A few years ago while I was still in school, I was just sitting in my dark room while my grandparents were downstairs, when out of nowhere, I felt a soothing presence in my dark room wrapping around me in a hug, his wings encasing me.

"At first I thought the window was open but it wasn't. I asked who he was and he said, 'Michael.' I like to think of him of my guide and guardian angel. St. Michael, after being called, saved me on two separate occasions, from demonic possession in August 2015. I never met my Animal Guide yet but I hope to. My grandmother, who passed six years ago, is also my Guardian Angel. My guides not only communicate with me, ghosts of pets and people do as well. I see my aunt's late black Pepper each time I visit her or vice versa," she said.

Chasity Ramirez Henderson also hears and feels her guides by utilizing her metaphysical gifts. "I hear a chirpy, static noise, or feel a tingle of energy on the side of my body," she said. "I've seen flashes of images in mind's eye. I've also had songs come on at the right time," she said.

People communicate with their Spirit Guides in a variety of ways. Instead of always feeling them one specific way, they get multiple prompts.

Other Ways of Feeling Your Guides

People are unique to one another. How one person interprets the signs is often different from how someone else experiences it. People often feel their guides in a variety of ways too. You might get a mixture of methods, providing you're open to the communication.

Jerry Lister's Story

For me Spirit Guides are felt and/or experienced in a few ways. Oftentimes after saying a prayer for a special intention, I will ask for a sign, especially if I have asked one who has passed on to intercede for me.

If it is my Dad, then soon after asking for a sign, I'll be compelled to turn on the radio and, lo and behold, a Frank Sinatra song will just begin playing. Frank was my Dad's favorite artist.

On those occasions where I may be praying for a child who is ill or dealing with a malady, I will ask a friend's daughter who died of

SIDS to intercede for me. Usually within a day of asking for such intercession, I will have a monarch butterfly land on my shirt. This is a sign that she has passed on my message to a Power bigger than myself....my God. It could be the dead of winter and a butterfly will appear and interact with me. This is a definite sign.

There are also many incidences of cardinals showing in my back yard and perching themselves on my weeping willow tree or my deck railing immediately after speaking to my Mom who passed in 1983.

There are also physical incidences where a ceiling fan or a light will turn itself on after me mentally thinking of something and I'm seeking confirmation of that thought. Those incidences are too frequent to be just a coincidence. And then there are those times where you just all of a sudden get a gut feeling that something is wrong with a dear friend who lives far away. Where that thought comes from is unexplainable. But when you follow up and discover that there is indeed an issue or a concern, you validate that your Spirit Guide pushed you to make that call and help with suggestions. Some things in life are easily explainable, but there are those times where you know your call to action either thru prayer or a phone call are the direct result of being empowered by the Spirits who care for you and your friends.

***

Aprille Bernard's Story

I met Aprille Bernard years ago at the S.K. Pierce Haunted Victorian Mansion, which was the subject of my 2013 book *Bones in the Basement – Surviving the S.K. Pierce Haunted Victorian Mansion.*

Aprille Bernard often hears her spiritual allies speaking to her aloud. The messages come out loud and clear as they sit beside her or sit in the backseat of her car while she's driving. Sometimes, she even hears them in her sleep.

"I heard someone say 'Aprille..APRILLE!!' Bill heard it a few times and would wake up and say, 'Hunny, someone is trying to get your attention.' I would say okay and then fall back to sleep and they would be in my dream to tell me whatever they needed to let me know."

After her long-time love, Bill Wallace, passed away, she began getting messages from him, as well.

"I had a situation recently. I went out to my car and heard Bill clear as a bell say, 'Watch yourself!' The message helped her get through a potentially uncomfortable situation and gave her the confirmation she needed.

Animal Guides often appear near her stomach. She has identified several Animal Guides, including cats, dogs, ravens, a ferret, an owl, a wolf and a deer. "The animals have been there mostly as a soothing thing. When I am sick, sad, etc., they will come to me," she said.

***

Scarlett McGrady feels her spiritual ally wrap himself around her. The sensation is warm and heavy in the middle of her upper back between her shoulder blades. "My guides are like thoughts that I know are not mine. Knowing without knowing," she said.

***

Debbie Decker has a female guide who has been with her for nearly eleven years. She feels her guide daily, sometimes two or three times in one day. "She travels with me on an airplane and goes with me in my car. She reads my mind and she taps or clicks on things so that I recognize her acknowledgement she's been seen," she told me.

One of Debbie's spiritual allies often manipulates items in her house, as well. "She used to tap on my keyboard," she said. Her guide would also turn on a lamp and pull items out from the covers and drop them on the floor, as well as mess with her tea kettle. She often hears taps and makes sounds with her plastic water bottles. "This might happen like four or five times an evening and it seems that she knows what I'm thinking and what

I'm doing," she said. She has also had several occurrences of her ally turning on the car radio while she's driving to let her know she's nearby.

***

Anthony Ortiz said, "For me, it comes through thoughts and vivid visions. Some come forward with very specific details and clarity, you feel the message...the rest is up to you."

***

Carmen Cluck has three Spirit Guides, as well as her late husband's guides. She also has several Animal Guides: one canine, three felines, two birds and one buffalo. She joked, "The bed gets really crowded."

***

Brittany Macomber shared an experience with me on how she connects with her Spirit Guides.

Brittany's Story

I am a Theta Healer, and I am also clairaudient and have always heard whispering and what not. Growing up, I never paid any attention to it but it scared me, so when I decided to pursue Theta Healing, my spiritual connection really became strong so now my guides are always right there to help me with anything.

Theta Healing is a process where a trained practitioner goes into a deep meditative state, using Theta brainwaves to reach a more relaxed state. Here, they can connect with their Spirit Guides easier and use them to help others.

"The latest thing to happen was I was about to have an anxiety attack and I felt something gently squeeze my hand. It distracted me, and so I was able to calm down," she said.

***

Psychic Medium Crystal Folz feels that a lot of people have contact with their Spirit Guides, but it's often easier to ignore them.

"They get these feelings and they know they need to do certain things. Their guides will keep pushing them and keep pushing them, but they avoid those things because it's easier to not do them," she said.

Despite how you feel your spiritual allies, it's important to use what you have to further your development. Ask them for a clear sign of their presence and then pay attention to the changes in your life.

When I'm in doubt, I pull out my pendulum and use it to help me clarify. Other people use meditation or other mind quieting activities to create a connection to their guides.

Why Guides Sometimes Resist Your Requests

Life would be so easy if we had someone to make all our decisions for us, wouldn't it?

We'd never have to worry about what to do next. We'd just ask our guides and they would give us all the answers. Unfortunately, or perhaps fortunately, it doesn't always work that way.

Part of our reason for being here, living these lives, is to learn and grow.

When I was a child, I knew a girl who had an easy life. Her parents didn't make her do any chores and she was allowed to come and go as she pleased. When she did something wrong, her parents looked the other way and made excuses for her behavior.

As you can imagine, this girl grew up and was released into a world she wasn't prepared for. She no longer had her parents there to pave a clear path for her. She was presented with obstacles she wasn't capable of dealing with. She ended up becoming addicted to drugs and alcohol, wasn't able to hold a full time job and ended up in and out of jail for most of her life.

I believe that one of the greatest misconceptions we embrace is that life is supposed to be easy. Life isn't supposed to be easy. It's supposed to be difficult. That's how we learn.

The true key is learning how to use these difficult experiences to our benefit. When something horrible happens to you, instead of latching onto the pain, anger and sadness, flip it around. Ask yourself, "What did I learn from this?"

The rear view mirror method is often a good learning tool for this, as well. After Skeeter Wellhouse shattered her ankle, it acted as a catalyst to propel her forward.

"I came out of it with a drive to finally focus on me, not just putz and dream and wish, but putting foot to pavement. I got serious about my health, my work as a psychic, getting my family out of New Mexico and rebuilding my family. It was as if I had broken the shell of the old me and just absolutely was reborn when they finally took off that cast," she said.

For Sue Collins, one door closed so another could open. After working for the same company for thirteen years, in what she considered her dream job, she was suddenly laid off. "I was devastated but soon landed an even better job. I have been there for 10 years now and love it more every day," she said.

Duckie DuBois shared a story that demonstrates this perfectly.

Duckie's Story
About eight years ago, my husband got a job offer in another town. We would be an hour from both our families, but the offer was too good to pass up.

While we were excited about the prospects, this meant that our home was going to be left vacant. At the same time, our son, who was married with three children, put their home up for sale. Their house sold really fast, which left them homeless, so they moved into our vacant home.

Within two months of living there, his wife decided she didn't want to be married anymore and left our son alone with three children, one being just a baby. Now, I'm an hour away and devastated, but we couldn't leave our situation or my husband wouldn't have had a job. It became a nightmare.

I kept asking God why he moved me away at such a horrible time. I felt like we made a huge mistake. To make matters worse, our daughter recently married and got transferred with her army husband to Texas. Then, to top it off, my sister got breast cancer.

My husband and I managed to get my sister to every chemo appointment. I stayed with her for the four hours of treatment and he would drive back almost two hours each way to get us.

Afterwards, I would have to leave her at home and go back the next day. We did this for months.

Then, as if this wasn't enough, my mother-in-law got colon cancer. During this time, we would drive our grandchildren to doctor's appointments, to school plays, etc., all an hour's drive each way.

I gained a lot of weight during this time because the stress was so bad. Our son was almost working around the clock.

About four years ago, our son ended up doing landscaping and started doing a job closer to where we lived. Some people where we lived met him and told him about a young woman who worked for them, who was going through a bad break up. They thought she would be a perfect match for our son. I said, "Well, let's see what happens."

They came back again that next summer and brought her with them. They invited our son out to dinner with them. Well it was love at first sight for both them! Our son had also just gone through another bad break up as well so I guess they had a lot in common.

She lived in New York and he lived in Maine. Even though they talked on the phone as friends frequently, after six months they knew they wanted more. Our son soon moved his family to New York.

We now have an amazing daughter-in-law. Our three grandchildren have the mom they deserve and she has a sweet little girl who is now our granddaughter. It's pretty much worth everything we all went through. My son says he would do it all again just to be with her. And, another twist, my sister survived the cancer and now has a job making great money working with the housekeeper where we live! I feel like I can finally enjoy my time at the ocean.

***

Duckie's story shows great insight into the rear view mirror approach. By looking back, we can see the reasons for some of the things that happened to us and make better sense of them.

Only your Spirit Guides and your Higher Self know the intricacies of your purpose in this lifetime. Your lesson could be as simple as learning humility or as complicated as paying off a karmic debt from a previous incarnation. Or, it could be a combination of many aspects.

Sometimes it's difficult to understand the reasons why we experience what we do and why life is often difficult. We aren't born with our soul contracts in our hands, providing us with a map to follow. We have to figure it out ourselves.

Looking at the Signs

Most people will see patterns in their lives that help them understand their soul contract. Lessons will be given to us over and over again until we learn them.

For me, handling conflict seems to be a theme. I have never been very good at conflict resolution. My preferred method of dealing with big issues is to run away from them and hope they'll go away. On a conscious level, I understand this isn't the best way to handle life's issues, but that doesn't make it any easier.

The lessons have been clear. When I was married, my husband and I rarely fought. We employed a passive aggressive approach to our conflicts, something that only served to make things worse. We eventually divorced because we seldom talked about the things that bothered us.

It wasn't until I started working full time as a manager that I learned to handle conflict. I saw the implications of letting a situation go unresolved. I learned to break down each conflict and find a productive way to solve it. This taught me how to deal with the conflicts in my personal life. Once I started meeting my problems head on, the steady stream of conflicts seemed to ease up. I'm not saying I'm perfect at it, but I have learned to be open and honest and to stop running away when I don't like what I'm seeing.

If you don't know what your soul contract involves, spend some time meditating on it. Ask your guides for clarification and begin to inspect your life. What are the things that bother you? What seems to reappear over and over again? These are the issues you need to work on.

Until you work on resolving your issues, they will keep coming at you, one after another. Take responsibility for it and accept it as part of your life's path, then start working on how to better handle it.

When Life Lessons are Difficult

There are times when we experience traumatic events to help us better learn a message. The more traumatic the lesson, the more important it is for us to learn from it.

One of my friends, who I'll call Alicia to protect her privacy, shared a story with me that demonstrates this perfectly.

Alicia owns a pet sitting business, one that takes great strides to provide the best care for her clients and their pets. I've known Alicia for decades and consider her to be one of the most compassionate, loving people I've ever known. She is the kind of person who will shoo a fly outdoors to avoid killing it.

Alicia's life had become incredibly overwhelming. After nursing her long-time love through a terrifying health issue, they took a trip to Alaska to celebrate his recovery. Once they returned, work had piled up and Alicia found herself attempting to dig out.

She often picked up pets and either escorted them to another doggy daycare facility or brought them back to her home, where they spent the day with her.

On this morning, she picked up five dogs. Two were going to doggy daycare and the other three were coming home with her. It was already a hot day, with the temperatures soaring into the eighties at nine in the morning.

She dropped the two dogs off at daycare and then headed home with her other charges.

One of the dogs coming to her house was a long haired German Shepard named Chance. Normally when she picked up Chance, she brought him to the doggy daycare, but since the day was supposed to be hotter than most, his owners asked if she would bring him home with her.

When she arrived home, she opened up the door to let the dogs out. She was exhausted and was looking forward to having the rest of the day off. When she opened the door and encouraged the dogs out, she didn't realize she'd left Chance in the car.

She brought everybody in and started her day then realized she'd forgotten Chance in the car. With panic lacing through her veins, she raced out to the car and discovered Chance.

He was limp and unresponsive. She tried to do CPR and cool him down, but it was too late. Chance had died.

Alicia's life took a downhill spiral at that point. She didn't eat for four days and ended up in the emergency room for intravenous fluids.

"I couldn't even look people in the eye. It was a long drawn out process, healing and therapy – dealing with the PTSD," she told me. Even though she knew it was an accident, she didn't feel as though she deserved any happiness, but she knew she needed to "own it." She contacted all of her clients, veterinarians she's worked with and her friends and told them what happened so they wouldn't hear it from someone else second hand.

Three years have passed and Alicia is slowly healing. The people who were her closest friends stopped associating with her. Although the experience was traumatic, she learned many lessons from it. She has learned to embrace change more than she did. She set up protocols to help her run her business safer and more efficient. She became stronger with her partner and no longer puts up with toxic people.

She still has a tremendous amount of guilt, but knew she had to find a way to live her life and learn from the lesson.

Honoring Your Spiritual Allies

I am always thankful for everything my spiritual allies have done for me. I feel them on a daily basis and they've helped me through some difficult situations, bringing me to a place of peace and acceptance. How do you even go about thanking someone for doing that?

I've been told that they don't need to be thanked. They do what they do willingly and graciously. That's why they're here. While I understand and appreciate that, I still like to take time to honor them.

Everyone has different methods, depending on their faith and practices. For me, it's simple. I found something that resonates with me and I use it.

Offerings

I have many friends who follow the Pagan belief system. Through this, I've learned that making offerings to the allies who assist us furthers their ability to help us. I will often light a white candle or burn incense as my way to thank them for all they do. As I light it, I always say, "I light this candle (or burn this incense) as an offering to my spiritual allies to thank them for all they do for me."

If you are making an offering to a deceased loved one, provide them with something that will be meaningful to them. Something as simple as showcasing a framed photo of them is meaningful. Or you might cook a meal that your loved one once enjoyed and set an extra plate at the table in honor of them.

Sometimes, we make these offerings without realizing it. My grandmother always loved anything lemon flavored, something that was passed down to me. Whenever I eat lemon pound cake, I think of Nanny and silently thank her for always being with me. Through my pleasure, she receives pleasure as well.

Prayer

Despite your religion, you can say a small prayer to your spiritual allies and higher powers to thank them. My prayers are often said quickly, but with gratitude, throughout the day. When I'm provided with a particularly valuable insight, I will often close my eyes and give thanks.

Perhaps the best way to honor your spiritual allies, is to put their guidance to work.

Using What You Learned

Over time, I've learned that there is a tremendous difference between religion and spirituality. Like many people, I was raised in a traditional structured family situation that involved going to church every Sunday.

As I sat there on the uncomfortable bench, listening to stories from the Bible that I wasn't fully convinced were more than fables, I began to wonder if this was the only way for me to connect with God.

For me, being in the middle of a forest brings me closer to God and my spiritual allies. Religion is the structure for this interaction, but spiritualism is how you are impacted by the connection. I found that by walking among the towering trees and lavish greenery, I could quiet my mind and just make a connection. As I did this, I silently thanked my maker and allies for all they provided me with, good and bad.

Some people need the safety net of religion, instead of attempting to walk a tight rope without something to catch them in case they fall. One of my students at my Paranormal 101 classes once said, "Imagine the chaos that would happen if there wasn't any religion." His words struck a chord with me.

What if there wasn't a Hell? Like Psychic Medium Brandie Wells, I don't believe in Hell either, at least not in the traditional fire and brimstone version. I believe that all souls go to Heaven, despite what they did on the earthly plane. I use this philosophy frequently when I'm doing house cleansings, trying to move lost souls into the light. "God loves you and you're welcome in Heaven," I tell them, which frequently eases their anxiety.

Hell is a concept similar to the principal's office or a maximum security prison. I believe it is man-made and powerful. It has certainly kept many people from doing things they knew they shouldn't do. Without it, as my student pointed out, the world would be in chaos.

If we did something horrible in our lifetimes, we right those wrongs through Karma. If you wrong someone or do something truly horrific, you will pay for it eventually, but your higher power doesn't just lock you up and forget about you.

Through my interactions with my allies, I've learned that the Golden Rule is the most important thing I could ever latch onto.

"Do unto others as you'd have them do unto you," it says. If we could all embrace that philosophy and treat everyone else we encounter in the same way we'd like for them to treat us, it would create a divine universe where we could all thrive. I realize this could never become a reality. There is a balance of good and bad that needs to be followed, but by providing as much light and love as possible, we can all make an impact on the world as we know it. I honor my allies by passing on this message as frequently as possible.

Be the Light

Through understanding our connections with other people, who we might have spent past lives with, we can have a better grasp on why we experience the things we do.

If something bad happens to you, don't make it your new mantra, learn from it. That's what our guides want us to do. This has helped me through many dark times. When something bad happens to me, I try to always find the lesson in it and use it to my benefit. When something good happens to me, I embrace it and give it as much power as possible, so it will help manifest even more greatness.

Our goal here on the earthly plane isn't to accumulate the most wealth, popularity and power as possible. Our goal is to make our souls the best they can possibly be.

By always looking for the bright side, you create a positive ripple that continues on and on, touching many people. Not only do you improve your emotional well-being, you pass this light onto others who also might need it.

I believe that out of all the messages we receive, that one is the one they want us to remember the most.

Contact Information

Psychic Medium Brandie Wells can be found at
http://brandiewells.com/

Shaman Michael Robishaw can be found at
http://www.michaelrobishaw.com/

Psychic Medium Barbara Williams can be found at
https://barbarawilliamsphd.com/

Licensed Mental Health Counselor Leslie Kim Herrington
Matilainen can be found at
https://lkm9092.wixsite.com/lesliematilainen

Author Gare Allen can be found at https://gareallen.com/

Continue Reading for an excerpt of *Dark and Scary Things – A Sensitive's Guide to the Paranormal World*

DARK

and

SCARY THINGS

By

Joni Mayhan

Introduction

Ghosts have always been a part of my life. When I was a child, I would lay in my bed at night watching the shadows dart across my ceiling.

Indiana summers were always hot and stifling, with the briefest of breezes drifting through the open window, causing the curtains to dance gently, swaying like ghosts in the moonlight.

Even though I was only a child of six, I knew enough about the physical world to understand that shadows weren't supposed to move unless something was causing them to do so.

The only light source in the room was a hooded nightlight plugged in beneath my window. It sent an amber glow of light splaying out in a half circle on my floor. I could see my stuffed animals, piled in the corner, their beady eyes reflecting in the light. It wasn't difficult to imagine them standing up on their wobbly legs and marching across the floor towards my bed.

I rolled over onto my back and again stared at the ceiling. It was mostly lost in darkness, but I could still see the dark silhouette of a shadow lurking in the corner. It wasn't shaped like a normal nighttime shadow. It was long and spindly, darker than the rest of the shadows. I stared at it for an eternity, my heart beginning to race as I realized it wasn't normal.

As if taunting me, it separated from the corner and drifted across the ceiling, not stopping until it was directly over my bed. I imagined it dropping from the ceiling and leaping onto the foot of my bed where it would skitter up to where I lay trembling. I pulled the blankets over my head and pressed my eyes tightly together, trying to remember the prayers they taught us in Sunday school. The only one I could remember ended with, "if I should die before I wake, I pray to God my soul to take," which didn't help me at all.

When I asked my parents about it, they did what most parents of the era did. They told me there was no such thing as ghosts and ushered me back to bed.

Unfortunately, simply dismissing the notion wasn't enough to make the ghosts go away. They followed me through every chapter of my life, in some fashion or another.

As I got older, I began to realize that other people didn't see these things. The shadows on their ceilings didn't move on their own, and they didn't get the maddening feeling that someone was watching them. The darkness became my worst enemy, and I feared going to bed each night. I also learned to stop talking about it, because people often gave me odd scrutinizing looks when I did.

People who saw shadows move were sometimes lumped together with people who heard voices in their heads. I knew I wasn't crazy, but I also knew this wasn't normal.

Eventually, I learned how to look away when I saw them, focusing on things that gave me comfort instead. It wasn't until I was an adult with two kids of my own that I finally came to grips with my unwanted gift. I was a sensitive. I could feel and hear when ghosts were nearby. Unfortunately, once I tapped into that ability, they began flocking to me in droves.

They've followed me ever since, hovering in the corner, waiting for the chance to pounce on me. Even as an adult, I still sleep with a nightlight, not because I'm afraid of the dark, but because I'm fearful of the dark and scary things that hide within it.

It's taken me years to understand why this is happening to me. For whatever reason, I was singled out and was given a gift that would perpetually shape my very existence. I could be a mother, a writer, a friend, but beneath it all, I'll always be a sensitive. Ghosts will always be a part of my life.

I am a beacon. My inner light shines so brightly, it attracts the world of the dead, drawing them in like moths to a candle flame. Ghosts see me and can't resist the pull. It's like gravity to them and they are helpless to avoid it.

As an adult, I am better equipped to handle the sensation than I was as a child. I have an arsenal of logic and explanations to use in my defense. I retreat into my bedroom each night, often falling asleep with the light on so I can see every inch of my room if I awaken suddenly from a nightmare.

I quickly discovered that I couldn't ignore it for long, because they would simply up the ante. If I looked away when I saw the dark shadows, strange thumps would sometimes pound on the wall beside my bed. During the daylight hours, when things seemed more manageable, items began disappearing and then reappearing in odd places. My pets became fearful of being in the house.

Sometimes the terror was so mind-numbing, I fled my bedroom, hoping to find sanctity in my living room. If I was lucky, I had a few minutes alone, but it didn't last for long. Soon, I would hear the strange ear ringing sound that signified their presence. Then, I would feel the icy cold blast of negative energy, filled with horrid thoughts and screaming protests. It was clear to me that if I didn't find a way out of the situation, they would eventually be my undoing.

I began searching earnestly for help. I soon began researching the phenomena with fervor, learning as much as possible because knowledge is power.

I found several psychic mediums who were willing to help me, but none of them could pinpoint why these dark entities were following me home.

"You have a type," one medium told me, referring to the fact that all the entities looming in my house were disturbed men with a dark agenda. They might have been pedophiles, serial rapists, or men who put knives into other people while grinning maniacally. This didn't help me when day faded to night.

I joined groups on social media. I reached out to mediums and paranormal experts, only to be given the vaguest of answers.

My father always told me, "What doesn't kill you, makes you stronger," and I found this to be true. Despite the trail of ghosts that were numbering in the double digits, I fought back

Things got worse before they got better, but I learned a thing or two in the process. I want to share this information with others, in hopes it helps people like me who are trapped in the shadows between the living and the dead.

In October of 2014, I began teaching a Paranormal 101 class in the town of Gardner. Due to the success of my true paranormal books, *The Soul Collector, Devil's Toy Box, Ghostly Defenses,* and *Bones in the Basement,* people were curious about the world of the dead. Initially, it was a way to make a little extra grocery money, but it became something altogether different.

I met some truly wonderful people who have become more like family. Through the classes, I've learned as much as I've taught. The students quickly surpassed their teacher and we founded a union that will stand the test of time.

(From Chapter 1)

The Devil's Hour

As the clock approaches the hour of 3AM, something strange happens in the world around us. The veil between the living and the dead grows thinner, allowing free passage between the two dimensions. Demons, ghosts and interdimensional creatures slip into the land of the living, creating havoc and tormenting us as we lay in bed sleeping. They call it the Devil's Hour or sometimes, the Witching Hour.

Some people find themselves waking up every night during the Devil's Hour, feeling a chill in the air as though they aren't alone. They might awaken from a nightmare that seems all too real, only to find themselves face to face with their night stalkers. Many believe it's more than just lost souls wandering our plane of existence, that it's the work of demons who are mocking the Holy Trinity of the Father, the Son, and the Holy Ghost. Since Jesus Christ supposedly died on the cross at 3PM, they use the opposite hour to torment the living in the same manner they might hang crosses upside down.

Many paranormal researchers have sworn by the Devil's Hour for years, claiming that ghostly activity is often heightened between the hours of 3 and 4AM. One paranormal television show once referred to it as "dead time," focusing the majority of their investigation during that time period. Others are more skeptical about the concept. After all, how do ghosts and demons account for Daylight Savings Time and all the various time zones?

As it turns out, there might be a reasonable explanation for the heightened paranormal activity.

Personally, I've always been skeptical about the Devil's Hour. As a paranormal investigator and sensitive, I've experienced activity at every hour of the day and night. There doesn't seem to be a reason for one hour of the day to be more active than any other hour. I've seen apparitions in the early hours of the morning and have watched shadow people dance across the room at midnight. As a sensitive, I can feel and hear them as they move around the room. They don't tend to abide by our preconceived notions of what a ghost is supposed to do. Their ability to be unpredictable is one of their best cloaking abilities. If we knew precisely when and where to find them, we would quickly solve the mystery of the ghost world. Could we be empowering them?

Anyone who has spent more than a minute researching paranormal protection methods knows that the best protection is the belief you put behind it. It doesn't matter if you're using religious medals, semi-precious stones or salt from the ocean, if you believe it's going to protect you, you are giving it more power to help you. On the other side of the concept is the belief that something can and will hurt you. By giving negative entities their very own time slot for tormenting us, we could be encouraging the behavior by giving it more energy to be successful.

Another theory of mine regarding the Devil's Hour revolves around what happens to me as I start to drift off to sleep.

It happens every night. As my brain waves slow down, bringing me closer to the place where dreamland reaps, I feel the ghosts in my house drift closer to me. Sometimes, it seems as though they are lurking at the corners of my room, waiting for that precise moment. There might actually be a scientific reason for this.

As we fall asleep, our brain waves slow down, dropping us from the Beta Stage, which is fully awake, to the Alpha Stage, which is when we are just beginning to relax, to the Theta Stage, which is the gateway between wakefulness and sleeping. The next step is the Delta Stage, where we are fully asleep and begin to experience REM (Rapid Eye Movement) sleep. As we sleep, we move through the stages, one by one, over and over again.

Mediums have long suspected that ghosts and spirits are able to communicate with us better when our minds are more relaxed. As our brain waves slow down, either through meditation or sleep, we turn off the parts of our brain that processes reason. In a sense, all of our self-doubt and criticism is disabled, as though a switch has been thrown. During the Theta Stage, our minds are ripe for communication. We aren't fully asleep, leaving the door cracked open a bit. If our brains cycle through the sleep stages throughout the night, it would stand to reason that we might hit the Theta Stage at 3 AM, depending on our own individual sleep cycles. If you are one of those people who wake up at 3AM every night, feeling as though you aren't alone, you might not be. Someone might have been attempting to communicate with you. Cheery thought, I know.

Another theory follows the natural sleep process our bodies go through every day. We aren't usually aware of it, but we are programmed like well-oiled machines. Our bodies perform a specific way due to the amount of light they receive at specific times of the day. This is called the circadian rhythm. It's our body's' biological clock, so to speak. We are naturally programmed to wake up when the sun rises and to grow weary when the sun sets, even if our lives don't revolve around conventional schedules. When we approach our normal sleep time, a specific group of neurons called SCN (suprachiasmatic nucleus) send messages to regions in our brain that help us wind down and fall asleep, including an area of the brain called the pineal gland.

The pineal gland is a tiny pinecone shaped gland, located in the middle of our brains and controls the production of the sleep hormone melatonin. As our circadian clock approaches bedtime, this gland is stimulated to produce more melatonin. Interestingly enough, the pineal gland is also connected to our Third Eye Chakra, the hotspot for our psychic and mediumistic abilities.

This means that two things are happening: our inner skeptic is quieted while our intuitive abilities are being stimulated. This could happen at any hour, depending our normal sleep

schedule, but given that most people operate on a bedtime prior to midnight, they will typically get tired by 3AM. If they are paranormal investigators who are out on an investigation, chances are they will be getting tired by 3AM, considering most of us work daytime jobs and are normally asleep by that time.

While this information provides some explanation for why some people might sense more paranormal activity, it doesn't explain everything. People who are on different sleep schedules probably won't be impacted by the Devil's Hour, yet many still claim to experience heightened activity. This brings me back to the empowerment theory, making the entire concept of the Devil's Hour circular and returning.

Perhaps there is more to the Devil's Hour than what science can explain.

Maybe, it's exactly what we think it is. Either way, it's not something I'd recommend contemplating in the wee hours of the morning, especially not between the hours of 3 and 4AM.

Night Hag Syndrome

Jason woke up every night feeling pinned to his bed. The terror was very real. He could feel an unknown presence looming above him in the darkness. His hobby of photography had recently taken him to several reportedly haunted locations. Did something follow him home?

Jason has always been intrigued by abandoned buildings. A recent road trip with a handful of fellow photographers brought them to several paranormal hotspots. They spent a few hours at each location, focusing on the architecture and scenery. While he didn't necessarily get any creepy vibes while shooting the location, he still worried that something might have tagged along for the ride. What else could have woken him up in the middle of the night? The possibilities are as follows:

1. Sleep Paralysis

According to sleep researchers, a phenomena known as Sleep Paralysis, also called Old Hag Syndrome can cause you to become paralyzed while waking. When we fall into REM sleep, our bodies automatically paralyzes themselves, with the exception of eye movement and breathing. This prevents us from hurting ourselves while we dream. Acting out a dream of running or falling could create serious damage to ourselves or our bed mates if this didn't happen. In rare situations, sometimes the mind wakes up before the body does, which essentially paralyzes us, but leaves us fully aware. Some people who encounter this, also report the feeling of being watched or seeing something in the room with them. Many of them see an old hag-like creature sitting on their chests, pinning them to the bed. That's where the theory gets interesting.

Typically, people who research sleep issues seldom delve into the paranormal probabilities. It's far easier to explain a situation with proven scientific theories behind them than it is to blame it on something like ghosts, but it still bears discussion. Can ghosts actually cause sleep paralysis? Is there any truth behind the Night Hag concept?

According to psychic medium, Barbara Williams, there could be more to it than a medical condition.

"Yes. There can be cases of entities holding someone down. It may be rare, but people can have attachments and possession," she said.

2. Paranormal Entities

Ghosts can and will attach themselves to the living. While many of them roam the earth with no desire to interact with their living counterparts, many others have darker intentions. They latch onto the living, using them as energy food sources while finding delight in tormenting their days and nights.

In Jason's case, I asked him if he had any other experiences that could point towards a haunting, such as items disappearing, mysterious sounds in empty rooms or a feeling of being watched. Thankfully, he hadn't. That led me to another question. I asked him if he could sometimes control the direction of his dreams.

Was he lucid dreaming?

3. Lucid Dreaming

People who are able to control their dreams are lucid dreaming. By realizing they are dreaming, they can take their dreams in any direction they want to. Unfortunately, a side effect of this is inadvertent sleep paralysis. In Jason's case, he's had one experience where he was able to control his fear and fully wake himself up, which could be the start of lucid dreaming.

Understanding all the circumstances surrounding a Night Hag episode is essential to stopping the process from reoccurring. If this happens to you, do your homework and then work on finding a solution that fits your situation.

If it's truly a Night Hag, then you have your work cut out for you. Seek the assistance of an experienced psychic medium to help you clear your energy.

Dark and Scary Things – A Sensitive's Guide to the Paranormal World can be found where you purchased this book.

About the Author

Joni Mayhan is a paranormal investigator and author who has dedicated most of her life to the study and documentation of the paranormal world. After spending thirty years in New England, she recently relocated to her home state of Indiana where she is currently working on her next book.

To learn more about Joni, check out her website: Jonimayhan.com

Made in the USA
Middletown, DE
25 March 2017